insight text guide

Sue Tweg

Gattaca

Dir. Andrew Niccol

First published in 2002, reprinted 2003, 2005, 2008, 2009, 2011, 2012, 2013, 2014, 2015, 2016, 2017, 2019, 2021, 2023.

Insight Publications Pty Ltd
3/350 Charman Road
Cheltenham VIC 3192
Australia
Tel: +61 3 8571 4950
Fax: +61 3 8571 0257
Email: books@insightpublications.com.au

www.insightpublications.com.au

National Library of Australia Cataloguing-in-Publications entry:
Tweg, Sue
Insight Text Guide: Gattaca
ISBN 9781920693091
Insight Text Guide.
Bibliography.
For secondary school age.
791.4372

Other ISBNs:
9781925316339 (digital)
9781925316346 (bundle: print + digital)

Cover design: The Modern Art Production Group

Printed by Markono Print Media Pte Ltd

contents

CHARACTER MAP

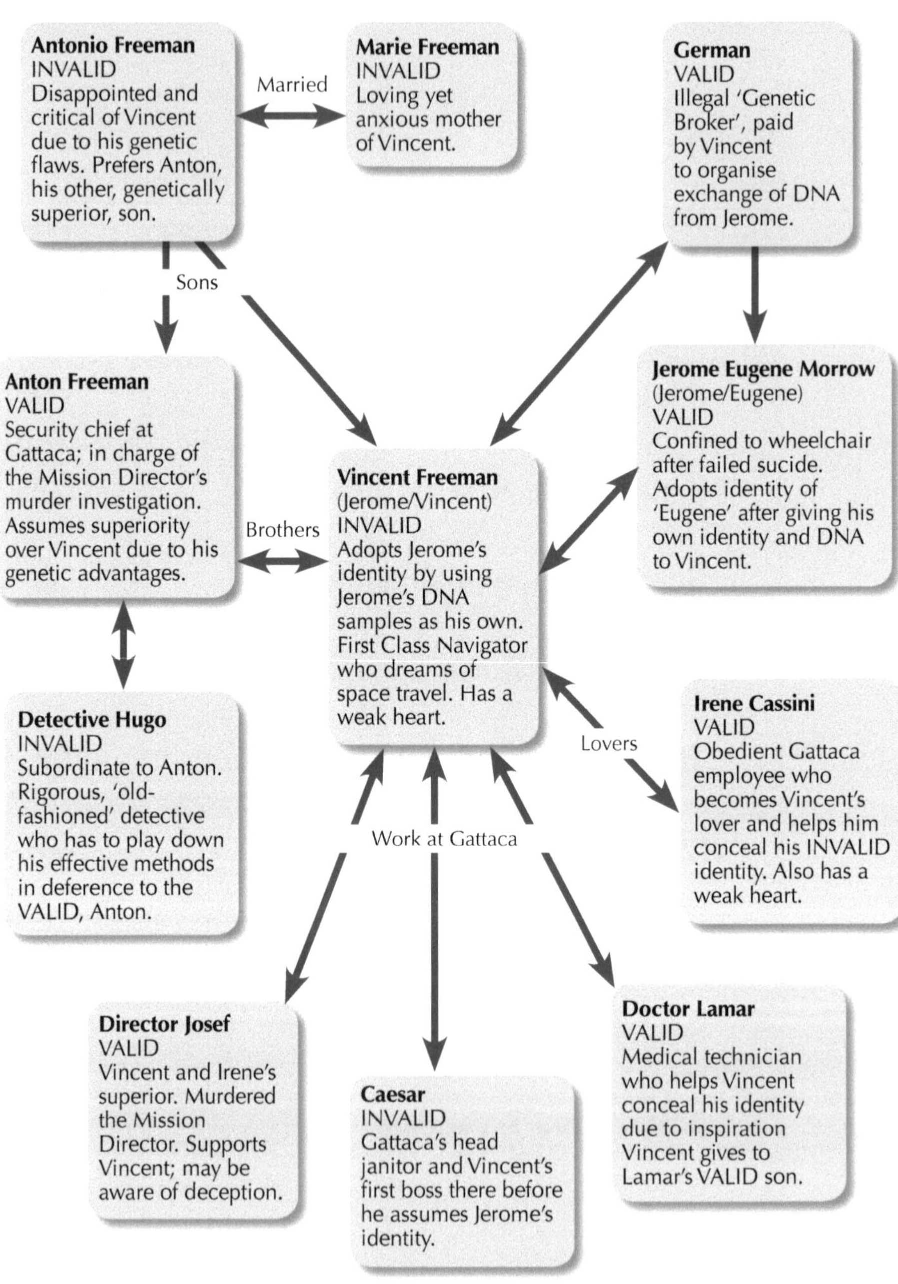

OVERVIEW

On a first viewing, you might describe *Gattaca* (1997) in simple terms as a classic **science fiction adventure** combined with a **crime story** (bold type is used throughout for important terms that are discussed later in the guide). Throughout the film we keep seeing how a relentless police search for a murderer is getting on. Our interest soon turns to another story about a young man called Vincent, known throughout by his workmates as 'Jerome'. We follow Vincent as he overcomes the supposed biological limitations he was born with to achieve his dream of becoming an elite astronaut in Gattaca Corporation's space program. In the process, we see how he is helped significantly by several other key characters.

The thematic connection between the two plot strands is not clear immediately, but we notice from the very beginning that they are twisted around each other visually in the *mise en scène*. This twisting interaction gives us our first clue to deeper themes and issues that make *Gattaca* such a fascinating, complex film for analysis. The spiralling narrative mirrors the spiral staircase centrally placed in Jerome's apartment, which connects Vincent with Jerome (and with Anton), and which, in turn, brings to mind the key spiral symbol for life itself that is at the heart of the whole story – **DNA (deoxyribonucleic acid)**, the **double helix** that carries genetic coding in all living things.

Gattaca, set in 'the not-too-distant future', is a fictional encounter with a society that is evolving through genetic engineering. The film explores key concerns for viewers in a 21st-century Western-industrial society. *Gattaca* gives us a model of society built on **eugenics** (a scientific program to improve the human breed) and demands that we think about it, challenging our concepts of '**human**' and '**individual identity**', and values.

INVALID Vincent may be prone to heart disease and an early death (according to his DNA test sample taken moments after birth), but in this story he triumphs with genetic help from Jerome/Eugene, who comes to share his spirit. So-called **VALID** people, genetically designed to be 'superior', suffer the pain of defeat. A central message of the film is that 'there is no gene for the human spirit' (in reality, this can't be known for certain at present).

Key point

Bear in mind these questions as you watch the film: 'What clues do we get about how society values its people?' and 'Does the society at all resemble the one we live in?'.

BACKGROUND & CONTEXT

Gattaca is set in a science-fiction world but is recognisably the United States on Earth in 'the not-too-distant future'. How does the film create this world for the viewer and what built-in values seem to be evident? Following, are two important ways to pursue ideas around the question of context.

Science with designer style

The everyday world outside the Gattaca complex looks grim for ordinary people, who seem to be either menial workers or drifters. The prospect looks brighter for the Gattaca elite, even though their environment seems functional and impersonal, lacking in comfort despite its expensive polished look.

A manned flight to a distant planetary moon is about to blast off but there's no clumsy astronaut gear in evidence. Both technology and scientists are calmly in control: above all, there is conspicuous surface 'style'. Like their flawless suits, men and women keep feelings buttoned up at Gattaca – or so it appears. This seems to be a science-world in a dream or virtual reality: where is the functioning laboratory or mission control centre? Computers analyse and manage every aspect of Gattaca's activity, while an army of drone-like cleaners deals with waste products.

Compare the screen images with *2001: A Space Odyssey* (1968), another key science-fiction film that was spectacularly stylish in both its visuals and its creation of a coolly efficient 'scientific' environment without much evidence of real-life science. At the heart of *2001's* story was an insane homicidal computer. In *Gattaca*, too, something deeply disruptive lurks in a perfectly structured environment. This is why the camera insists we keep looking at graphic shots of the murdered Mission Director's blood-covered head. Somebody has done the unthinkable – wielded a computer keyboard as a weapon. The flawless surface of Gattaca has been violated.

Recreating mythology

Arthur C. Clarke's story 'The Sentinel' is the basis for 2001, which ends with a Jupiter space mission controlled by a very advanced interactive computer, an artificial intelligence called HAL (try making another familiar name by advancing each letter in HAL's name by one place, IB ... ?). The mission has come about after humans finally reached a stage of scientific knowledge that left them intrigued by the meaning of a mysterious ancient monolith, a 'Sentinel' placed aeons ago by unknown extraterrestrials.

What impels Vincent in *Gattaca* is a desire to get off Earth and explore space. As he blasts off to Titan, he makes the significant comment that we 'were all once part of the stars. Maybe I'm not leaving ... maybe I'm going home'. If you choose, you can follow up this idea by reading *Cosmos* (1981), Professor Carl Sagan's brilliant account of how science and civilisation developed together. Sagan writes of 'the ash of stellar alchemy ... emerging into consciousness'. He continues:

> At an ever-accelerating pace, it invented writing, cities, art and science, and sent spaceships to the planets and the stars ... It has the sound of epic myth, and rightly ... (p.338)

> For we are the local embodiment of a Cosmos grown to selfawareness. We have begun to contemplate our origins: starstuff pondering the stars; organised assemblages of ten billion billion billion atoms considering the evolution of atoms; tracing the long

> journey by which, here at least, consciousness arose. Our loyalties are to the species and the planet. We speak for Earth. Our obligation to survive is owed not just to ourselves but also to that Cosmos, ancient and vast, from which we spring (p.345).

James Crick, the co-discoverer of the double-helix construction of DNA, would agree with Sagan's view but put it in less mystical-sounding terms. In conversation with Bryan Appleyard, Crick said:

> The end result of the human genome program on society will finally be to make people realise we are the products of evolution, not of a message from the sky. Finally they are going to find it impossible to ignore (Appleyard 2000, p.154).

There is, nonetheless, a strongly mystical underlay in the film that needs to be recognised. First, Vincent's mission is to Titan, the largest moon circling Saturn. This is an appropriate choice – even though the film's story is fiction – because, following *Voyager 1*'s encounter with Titan in 1980, scientific information about its atmospheric chemistry makes it a possible candidate for Earth-like evolution in the distant future.

'Titan' and 'Saturn' are names worth considering. In classical mythology, the Titans were a family of gods, sons of Uranus, the original creator god ('Father Time'). Cronos (like the Roman god, Saturn, and also a 'time' god), was a Titan: he overthrew Uranus and, in turn, was overthrown by Zeus, the leader of the next generation of young gods. This saga of young gods overthrowing old ones is all about the way succeeding generations surpass their elders in knowledge and skill. Both Uranus and Cronos tried to devour their children and were only prevented, and finally overthrown, by cleverness. Because time devours human beings, some people are already speculating about achieving 'immortality' through genetic intervention in the ageing process.

Vincent, then, is the young rocket-navigator hero going out to encounter powerful forces, genetic ones on Earth and unknown challenges in the cosmos. As the 'god-child' of mother Maria and protective 'father figure' Director Josef, his story may suggest an even more profound mythic base to some viewers.

Genes and genetics

Gattaca was made at the end of the 20th century, just as a huge debate in the media about the future direction and ethics of genetic manipulation (that had actually started in the 19th century) was firing popular interest. This debate will certainly continue and become more complex still.

Because it has vital implications for the life of every person and every living thing on Earth as well as being fundamental to the construction of the fictional *Gattaca*, you need to grasp a few names and basic genetic terms so that you can discuss issues thoughtfully.

This information has been edited from several sources (Nossal, Appleyard, Doherty), all noted in References & Reading at the end of this guide.

- **Genes** are the coded building blocks of all living things. The genetic blueprint for life is found in the **nucleus**, the control centre of every cell.
- The chemical building blocks of genes are made up of individual stretches of **nucleotides**. You'll be interested to discover that there are four base **nucleotides**, known by the letters **G A T C**. These are sequenced in triplets (G-A-A, followed by T-T-C etc, with many combinations possible). Single stretches pair up to create long **strands** of **DNA (dioxyribonucleic acid)**, twisted and interlocked like a zip fastener.
- DNA strands twist in a controlled way that always matches and bonds certain pairs of **nucleotide bases**. A **G** on one strand always pairs up with a **C** on the other, and an **A** with a **T**. Professor Nossal describes twisted DNA strands, the famous **double-helix** molecular structure, as 'circular staircase-like assemblies' – each step made up of a bonded pair of **bases**.
- Long stretches of paired bases in a double-stranded DNA molecule make up a **chromosome**. Each living species has a certain number of chromosomes, which code that species' individual characteristics. Every **human cell** has **46 chromosomes**.

Key point

Go to **http://www.dnaftb.org** This is a brilliant informative website with an animated primer on the basics of DNA, genes and heredity. You can look up the terms and see how things fit together in the double helix.

With the above information in mind, take a closer look at the film title and the opening credits design. Notice how each name emerges on the screen from the different combinations and placings of the four letters G A T C. All or some of these letters appear in every cast member's name. They are part of an alphabet – the common building blocks of names – as well as the markers of the four base nucleotides – the building blocks of DNA, joined in the double-helix molecule: Guanine, Adenine, Thymine and Cytosin.

It might be worth noting that the character name 'Jerome Morrow' lacks any of these letters, as though he is somehow inert or non-human, perhaps. A similar argument could be made for the cool murderer, Josef. However, the names Eu**G**ene ('well born'), Vin**C**en**T** ('successful one', someone who overcomes) and Freem**A**n, when combined, possess all the necessary components of the base code to make and continue creating life. Perhaps they will combine to bring life to Irene, another imperfect VALID whose name is also missing the key letters.

Genetics

Genetics is the study of genes, the biology of heredity. Geneticists are interested in questions about how organisms grow and function as they do. The double-helix biochemical structure of the DNA molecule was finally arrived at by Crick and Watson and their research team at Cambridge in the mid 1950s, although other scientists had been working on the same problem decades before.

The Human Genome Project is an initiative that has just completed mapping the entire gene-sequence of DNA, but – and this is crucial for *Gattaca* – scientists still don't know what it all means. So far they can be (cautiously) confident about the function of about a third of the genes in the total gene pool. A **genome** is complex and precious: it is the total 'map', or coded sequence, of genes that determine what an organism will be like. A human being has about 30,000 genes coding for basic proteins (about the same as white mice, compared to worms, that have 18,000, and plants, about 26,000).

Eugenics

Eugenics is the science of producing genetically superior beings through controlled breeding. The notion of improving the human species, given the political and social structures to implement this, is an ancient idea – and full of moral and ethical issues. At its most ruthless it led to Nazi extermination camps, ethnic cleansing, sterilisation programs and stolen children.

An example of eugenics working at a personal level could be seen in somebody choosing a sexual partner to have children with because of good looks, intelligence or perceived strength, or because the partner could be guaranteed not to be carrying some terrible **hereditary disease**. Serious diseases and birth defects were recognised as hereditary (carried within families) long before the concept of genetic carriers in DNA had been imagined. So the issue of choosing breeding partners carefully has always been significant to some people for the obvious reason, at least to them, that it is better for everyone concerned to avoid having babies who are certain to be born to suffer.

The issue is an ethical minefield. *Gattaca* offers some comments through the ways in which Vincent and Anton are conceived. INVALID Vincent's admission that he's a 'god-child' embarrasses Irene because, to her, his parents have behaved irresponsibly. His resumé is in his cells, as he says, and so he is discriminated against in education and job-choice. Even VALID Anton was engineered with a degree of 'chance' features, while Jerome's genetic makeup was rigorously engineered to give him every advantage. How realistic is *Gattaca*'s scenario for **designer babies**? Arthur Caplan describes 'The California-based Repository for Germinal Choice, known more colloquially as the Nobel Prize spermbank', which:

> has assigned itself the mission of seeking out and storing gametes from men selected for their scientific, athletic or entrepreneurial

> acumen. Their sperm is made available for use by women of high intelligence for the express purpose of creating genetically superior children who can improve the long-term happiness and stability of human society (Caplan 2001, p.64).

Long before genetic engineering became a science, Francis Galton (Charles Darwin's cousin) published his study of *Hereditary Genius* (1869), which advocated 'careful selection' to breed in 'desirable characteristics' and avoid 'dysgeny' – a decline in human 'quality'. You can see the fundamental problem: what precisely do these terms mean? And who decides?

Genetic engineering

Genetic engineering is the technology by which genes can be identified, isolated, turned on or off, snipped out of the DNA strand and reinserted somewhere else, or otherwise modified to combat disease or defects. Fired by media hype on the latest breakthrough, it is easy for ordinary people to assume that genetic engineering is about to make huge medical advances. Dolly the sheep was cloned in 1997 and stem cell research is currently handling tiny replicating bits of 'immortality'. Cloning has already raised anxieties about issues of individuality, while stem cell research has other ethical implications.

The significant thing to remember is that the way our genes work together is only partly understood at the present time. Genetic engineers recognise that they must be cautious about manipulating genetic material because they can't know the subtleties of gene interaction. One bit of DNA may not seem to be doing much *but* it could be fundamental to another gene's activity. Some **redundancy** appears to be built into the code (unknown, repeated or apparently duplicated chunks of material) but that doesn't mean that information coded is insignificant, just unknown.

Hence the big debate about good and bad genes – who knows exactly what genes do? Crudely stated, you could snip out, say, a bit of DNA carrying a hereditary defect (bad gene) but then realise that the very same gene in that position (good gene) was absolutely necessary to turn on another coded activity in the same system.

Key point

Considering the above information, think about Vincent, Anton and Jerome. What qualities does untampered-with Vincent have as a person (despite his apparent physical 'defects') that the other men seem to lack? Is their engineered DNA deficient in something perhaps?

Gen-ethics

Gen-ethics is an emerging branch of ethics focusing specifically on questions and problems looming on the horizon for genetic researchers and anyone else who has plans to utilise the results of genetic research commercially. 'Ethics' can be defined as the outcome of what principled members of a society would usually believe or do in relation to a particular, usually difficult, situation faced by that society as a whole. Ethical questions start with a phrase such as 'Is it right or wrong to … ' do or use something in order to get a certain desired result. Gen-ethics focuses on very sensitive issues of human and animal biological tissue use and on genetic modification of humans, animals, foodstuffs, plants and seeds.

Peter Doherty (*The Map of Life* [sound recording] 2001) touches on another key issue in the gen-ethics debate when he reminds us of non-scientific factors that contribute to a definition of 'human' being, leading our focus back to the gen-ethical context of *Gattaca*. First, Doherty points out that, 'The whole sequence of the human genome gives us no insight into the realm of the spiritual aspects of the human condition.' *Gattaca* publicity makes the same point more sharply: 'There is no gene for the human spirit.' Therefore, if the human spirit is not genetically determined and we consider one's individual spirit crucial in determining one's decisions and subsequent path in life, we must question whether being physically genetically engineered is actually that much of an advantage. This draws attention to the fact that **genetic determinism** – the belief that biology is destiny – may indeed be flawed.

Doherty goes on to explore the question of how 'good' people might act and behave in a situation where there is pressure from an 'evil' society

– what tensions operate on people in that sort of situation. In reference to this question, *Gattaca* supports the view that the intangible aspects of humanity – spirituality, love, respect, admiration, drive – override the tangible in not only determining what we make of our lives, but what we value and how this is reflected in our relationships with others.

Vincent knows he has deliberately become one of his society's **de-gene-erates**, marked as not just criminal but also morally corrupt for faking his genetic identifiers. He has outwitted the negative genetic resumé in his cells. He feels he's been forced into 'criminal' behaviour because his driving intelligence and cosmic vision refuse to be defeated by his biological makeup. While his society pays lip-service to equality, with **genoism** – discrimination on genetic grounds – being illegal, Vincent knows 'nobody takes the law seriously'.

Key point

If the central hero is de-gene-erate, so too are several key helpers who deliberately support 'Jerome', the elaborate genetic hoax. What motivates the real Jerome, Dr Lamar, German the genetic broker, Irene, Anton (reluctantly) and, possibly, Director Josef, to deliberately sabotage their eugenic community to protect Vincent?

Utopia or dystopia?

What kind of human environment is being depicted in *Gattaca*? Is it a **utopia** or a **dystopia**? These terms define fictional worlds (*u-topos*, 'no place') where social conditions are considered to be either perfectly organised and happy (**utopia**) or completely cruel and destructive to social happiness and freedom (**dystopia**).

You may have heard of *The Republic*, Plato's blueprint for a perfect state run by philosopher-rulers. It was a book that grew out of its times – war-torn, politically corrupt, 4th-century Greece. In 1516, Henry VIII's ill-fated Chancellor Sir Thomas More set out his own blueprint, entitled *Utopia*, for another kind of supposedly 'ideal' society. More's Utopia (an island somewhere in the 'new world') has a kind of benevolent community-policing that keeps everyone productive, while social policy is designed to ensure Utopians lead wholesome, cheerful lives.

The two best-known modern novels dealing with **dystopia** are George Orwell's *Nineteen Eighty-Four* (1949) and Aldous Huxley's *Brave New World* (1932). While Orwell describes a brutalising fascist regime in its full monstrosity, Huxley's fantasy is even more disturbing to read because it deliberately softens the effects of complete human domination with wry comedy as it describes a 'brave new world' population controlled by aggressive World State-controlled genetic manipulation. Almost at the end of the story, Huxley writes a showdown scene between the apparently benevolent World Controller and a dissident called 'Savage', who argues passionately for a world with human flaws – 'the right to be unhappy' – rather than a trouble-free enslavement of the human imagination.

Key point

Read Chapter 1 of *Brave New World*, which describes how new citizens are created in the laboratory from human eggs and sperm at the Hatchery and Conditioning Centre. Each developing embryo is subjected to chemical manipulation, which either stimulates its growth into an 'Alpha-Plus Intellectual' type or selectively damages DNA to produce different worker grades, down to strong but stupid 'Epsilon-moron' drones. The process is called Social Predestination. Although the tone is lighthearted, the issues raised by Huxley are deadly serious and connect directly with *Gattaca*. Then read Chapter 17, the showdown between Mustapha Mond and John Savage. Relate their argument to the VALID world view.

Huxley quotes a Russian philosopher called Nicholas Berdiaeff (1874–1948) to introduce his own dystopian story, because Berdiaeff raised a key issue about a life of freedom from utopian controls, posed in what sounded like a stupid question – how can utopias be prevented? He wrote (in French, my paraphrased translation):

> Utopias seem much more realisable than was formerly thought. And we find ourselves faced with a distressing question – how to prevent their concrete realisation? Utopias are realisable. Life moves towards utopias. Perhaps a new age is beginning, an age when intellectuals and cultivated folk will try to dream about averting utopias and returning to a non-utopian society, less 'perfect' and freer. (*Brave New World*, epigraph)

The society in which employees of the Gattaca Corporation enjoy high status is ideologically totalitarian, effectively a police-state controlling each individual from birth. It has not yet reached the ruined, polluted, slum state shown in *Blade Runner* (1982) and its mutants are the genetically privileged rather than crazed dregs or android experiments gone wrong of the earlier dystopian film.

Key point

Could Gattaca society be described as having any utopian features? Do you see any evidence of dissent in the community at large? Notice how most of the diners at the Cavendish Club respond when the police raid the premises, for example.

GENRE, STYLE & STRUCTURE

Genre

What kind of film is *Gattaca*? Several genres combine in this film and you should be able to recognise and comment on elements of each of them in your text analysis.

Science fiction

Be sure to take note of the 'futuristic' and 'retro' 1950s American science-fiction nostalgia in *Gattaca*'s *mise en scène*. Science fiction became popular in the cinema as Cold War anxieties of 'alien' (communist) invasion or takeover arose in the 1950s. Science fiction of this period is usually 'clean hands' science. Also, find *Things to Come* (1936), H.G. Wells' story filmed as a futurist scientific society growing out of the ruins of a catastrophic world war. *Gattaca* concludes with an effortless, high-tech, long-haul, space flight for its superman hero.

Crime story

Gattaca is a combination of 'police procedural' and film noir, with a 'mean streets' sense of corruption, lack of respect for individuals in the community and menace generated by law enforcers. Canny 'gumshoe' Detective Hugo demonstrates how attention to detail arrives at the correct homicide culprit who is not the chief suspect. References to police as 'Feds', 'Hoovers', 'J. Edgars' harks back to gangster-film America of 1940s–1950s (do your own research on J. Edgar Hoover, FBI). Note that there are several 'criminal' actions apart from murder that occur in the film, such as the falsifying of data, concealment and black-marketeering.

Love story

The thread of a love story runs through the film in two distinct strands, like another double-helix pattern. The first strand traces a developing relationship between Jerome/Vincent and Irene. How does love enter the equation when the societal emphasis is on genetically advantageous pairing? Irene is interested, but has Jerome/Vincent's DNA checked before pursuing a relationship with him. Conventional gender roles are maintained: even though Irene is a trained VALID astronaut, her weak heart prevents her from the space flight she desires. Instead, she stays Earth-bound and waiting, transferring her desire to her astronaut lover, Jerome/Vincent.

The second strand is less conventional, developing the intense bond between Vincent and Jerome, who share genetic data. In one brief scene, their charade to fool Anton allows them to share Irene, too. Their closer-than-fraternal bond is cemented when they set off together genetically into space.

A hero's life-story

Vincent's story, from childhood discouragement to rocket-navigator status is a classic 'ugly duckling' tale grafted onto a powerful American hero myth. Qualities of persistence, tenacity, vision, quick-wittedness, essential honesty (even though he uses his wits to cheat the Gattaca system) and brave spirit pay off for Vincent – and, by association, for his friends Jerome and Irene. The end of the film is Vincent's rite of passage into his new identity, a rebirth through the body fluids checkpoint and down the rocket boarding tunnel towards the stars, where he rides in his heroic chariot of fire, like a young god.

A morality play

A morality play is a form of drama, known worldwide and still performed in some places, that tells a story about human virtues and failings. In Europe it largely died out around William Shakespeare's time, although popular films today (including *Gattaca*) appeal strongly to audiences because their characters and plots follow the same kind of profoundly moving narrative tradition.

Characters in the past had symbolic names (such as 'Mankind', 'Wisdom', 'Everyman' or 'Good Deeds') and audiences got a clear message about ethical and moral behaviour that would lead to either eternal rewards or punishments.

One very famous play in this tradition, Christopher Marlowe's *Doctor Faustus* (1604), was based on a supposedly historical German scholar who signed away his soul to the devil in return for knowledge of the universe. In *Gattaca*, notice how Vincent, desperate to get into space, buys his VALID identity from a broker called 'German', who warns him that the commitment is binding. Unlike Faustus, who ended up cheated and in despair, Vincent achieves his goal and brings benefits to other people. *Gattaca* is the Faustus story turned into a positive morality play.

Style

The *mise en scène* of *Gattaca* is an interesting visual combination of two film styles. It morphs elements of film noir (darkness, shadows, surface tension and hard but opulent chrome/marble architecture for elite buildings) with hyper-cosmetic style, the glossy European look (flawless images, state-of-the-art digitals). One reviewer suggested that it seemed as if 'production decisions were made to strictly eugenic criteria' (Romney 1998, p.49).

Structure

Gattaca has a character-driven plot, with a lengthy flashback (Segments 6–17c) accompanied by the central narrator-protagonist's voice-over. Events rush together in a few key days before the Titan mission launch, charting the last stages in Vincent's struggle to achieve his dream.

Four tension-building plot lines interact and are successfully resolved:

- The search for a murderer, a race against time – crucial launch date set, which might be jeopardised by crime (and has been made possible *by* crime).

- Jerome/Vincent's successful evasion of authorities, including his brother: security chief Anton. Jerome/Vincent's true identity revealed to Gattaca at the last moment … and resolved by Lamar.
- The evolving love story. The relationship between Jerome/Vincent and Irene is temporarily resolved, suggesting a future for them both beyond the year's mission. Perhaps Irene will travel to the stars one day with Vincent.
- The evolving friendship across genetically set boundaries for Vincent and Jerome. Psychological and emotional growth for both men, redefinition of the meaning of 'brother' – is blood thicker than water, as the saying asserts? Is Jerome's death acceptable as part of the resolution?

SCENE-BY-SCENE ANALYSIS

For the purpose of analysis and discussion, the film has been divided into numbered segments, each with a descriptive title, and most with a number of individual but related scenes (marked a, b, c etc). Remember, this is only an outline. Always add your own notes on scene details that interest you. They will enhance your essay. The meaning of the film is conveyed to us structurally in two main ways, through *mise en scène* and editing.

Mise en scène

Mise en scène is 'that which is put into the scene', everything that is recorded in the frame by the camera – in other words, what there is to be perceived by the viewer at any one moment. Don't forget that lighting and sound (including music) contribute to the full effect of *mise en scène*. Sometimes in *Gattaca* you'll notice that the picture looks fuzzy or blurred – it's a deliberate effect, related once to Vincent's shortsighted point of view, but otherwise, to the idea that the story is nostalgic and about recalled memories.

Editing

Editing is the way **scenes** are constructed and joined together by careful **cutting** of the film into camera **shots** and consecutive **scenes**. Because a film has been edited, the viewer is able to link characters and construct a story. Notice how the extensive **flashback** sequence acts as a signal to the viewer, so that we know where we are historically in Vincent's life. He guides us further through sound, in his **voice-over** narration – it's as though he's remembering right now and telling us directly about his past.

Never underestimate the importance of the film editor (Lisa Zeno Churgin) as you 'read' the meaning of *Gattaca*. She worked with the director (Andrew Niccol) after the raw footage had been shot to create the smooth flow of the final film. Check for yourself how scenes change according to the use of different editing techniques, for example, **cutting** and **dissolving**.

Other film terms used in the following section refer to camera **shots**. Most are self-explanatory and they all help the viewer to construct meaning in the scene, for example, a **close-up** shot draws attention to significant detail, a **point-of-view** shot depicts a character's 'point of view', a **zoom-in** shot isolates detail, a **long** shot creates distance between the camera and the subject matter, a **tracking** shot directs the viewer's eyes to follow a specific path, and an **overhead shot** provides the viewer with a bird's-eye view (see Bordwell, D. and Thomason, K., *Film Art*, for a glossary of terms).

Segment 1: Opening credits sequence

Black screen to epigraph 1:

> Consider God's handiwork: who can straighten what he hath made crooked? Ecclesiastes 6.13

Black screen to epigraph 2:

> Sound begins … rumbling
>
> I not only think we will tamper with Mother nature, I think Mother wants us to. Willard Gaylin

FADE IN/ blue environment, identified not as natural sky, but blue-lit shower-cleanser-incinerator unit – future technology.

Opening credits begin, each name beginning as different combinations and placings of the letters **G A T C** (the **four basic nucleotides**: **G**uanine, **A**denine, **T**hymine, **C**ytosin).

Falling through blue space are two hugely magnified fingernail trimmings. The highly amplified impact of their landing is heard.

> Credits: E**T**h**A**n HAwke Um**A** **T**hurm**A**n

> Two strands of hair fall like heavy ropes.

MUSIC (sadly romantic, spiralling upward theme) begins with a strong surge as the title *Gattaca* appears on the screen: name made up of four key letters only.

> Eyelashes, shaving stubble and skin flakes fall like snow.

> Credits: Al**A**n **A**rkin Jude L**A**w **G**ore Vid**A**l Ernes**T** Bor**G**nine (list continues)

Gradually it emerges that Jerome/Vincent (Ethan Hawke), his name unknown as yet, is carefully shaving with a razor. Notice the extra close shave and the old-fashioned tool, the first of several 'retro' associations in the film. He is epilating, exfoliating himself in a display of super-hygiene – why? The camera voyeuristically observes him in close detail.

> Music credit: Mi**C**h**A**el Nym**A**n (music continues to build)

Segment 2: Jerome/Vincent's routine

2a) Establishing shot shows entire space. A young man steps out of a cleaning chamber, as out of a shower, and flames incinerate the 'debris' of his body. Notice the *mise en scène* stark functionality of the room and the shower-incinerator. DISSOLVE into an interior shot of the fridge containing stored pouches of blood and urine. A man straps a urine pouch to his leg and carefully attaches a sac containing a drop of blood to his thumb. DISSOLVE into a long shot of the room, showing the functional laboratory and domestic interior. CUT/

2b) Exterior. Day. Yellow light. Long shot of an apartment building (severely functional, bleak, featureless concrete, no 'nature' around), car leaving CUT/

Segment 3: Gattaca

3a) Exterior. Day. Establishing long shot of Gattaca Corporation building, lake in the foreground, trees CUT/

3b) Interior. Gattaca. Day. Futuristic and 'retro' environment, lots of concrete and chrome. Silent men in trilby hats (a noir 1950s image), sober-suited young men and women walk serenely, silently, up the elevator. Navy, grey, black tones. A young man approaches the elevator. CUT/

CAPTION OVER: The not-too-distant future

People queue for a thumb blood test at the identity-checking pad. A young man 'connects' with a young woman, Irene (Uma Thurman), her name unknown as yet, as he passes through the tester. She follows him. CUT/

Segment 4: Jerome/Vincent at work

4a) Interior. Day. Black screen. The camera tilts up, revealing a young man's face reflecting a computer screen image. He sits at his astronaut's workstation. The area is calm and quiet. He works intently at his console, which displays information on Saturn and its moon, Titan. A close-up shot of his keyboard shows him using a pocket vacuum cleaner to suck up all his bodily sheddings. As he's doing this, we observe Director Josef (Gore Vidal) walking up behind him, saying: 'You keep your workstation so clean, Jerome.' We hear the man's name for first time. Jerome/Vincent replies: 'It's next to godliness, isn't that what they say?' The Director picks up on the word 'Godliness' and muses a moment. He comments: 'I reviewed your flight plan. Not one error in a million key strokes … phenomenal … it's right that someone like you is taking us to Titan.' CUT/ a woman listening, her facial expression noted. Jerome/Vincent asks, 'Has the Committee approved the mission? There's been talk of a delay.' The Director responds, 'You shouldn't listen to talk ... you leave in a week ... you've got a substance test.' The Director leaves. Jerome/Vincent surreptitiously sprinkles body debris from a vial into his keyboard and places a hair strategically by the comb in his drawer. He does this methodically, drawing little attention to himself. CUT/

4b) Jerome/Vincent gives a urine sample. A conversation with the medical technician, Lamar (Xander Berkeley), follows, who refers to Jerome/Vincent's penis as a beautiful piece of equipment. He says, 'Don't know why my folks didn't order one like that for me.' It is said in jest, but this comment enables us to know that Lamar is genetically engineered. CUT/ a close-up shot of the test machine, which registers Jerome/Vincent as the VALID Jerome Morrow. Lamar casually asks Jerome/Vincent, 'Have I ever told you about my son?' He comments on Jerome/Vincent's calm demeanour, even though he's scheduled to go into space in a few days – isn't he just a bit excited? CUT/

4c) Interior. Day. Golden light. Jerome/Vincent stands at the window, looking out. Irene comes up the escalator and joins him. They watch the rocket launch through the glass roof. She is aware of his strong desire to go to space. Although he is outwardly calm, he watches every launch every day. She says, 'If you're going to pretend like you don't care, don't look up ...' and leaves.

Vincent's voice-over narration begins while watching another launch, walking along the corridors – noir style. Notice the *mise en scène*, with its angles and shadows. He says, 'The most unremarkable of events ... Jerome Morrow, Navigator First Class, is about to embark on a one-year manned mission to Titan, the fourteenth moon of Saturn ... a highly prestigious assignment. Although for Jerome selection was virtually guaranteed at birth. He's blessed with all the gifts required for such an undertaking ... a genetic quotient second to none. No, there is nothing truly remarkable about Jerome Morrow.'

All this is spoken as Jerome/Vincent approaches a corridor where a group of people are looking at something on the ground. He pauses by a window ledge. A point of view shot enables us to see what he sees – people looking down at the crushed head of a murder victim, lying in a pool of blood. His voice-over continues, '... except that I am not Jerome

Morrow.' Zoom-in to a close-up, blurred focus, golden light. MUSIC bridges to FLASHBACK/

Segment 5: Vincent's childhood

5a) Exterior. Establishing shot of palm trees, sunrise. The camera tilts down to a green car ('retro' 1950s style). Voice-over: 'I was conceived in the Riviera – not the French but the Detroit variety – in a car. They used to say that a child conceived in love has a greater chance of happiness. They don't say that any more.' Shot closes in on Vincent's parents embracing, asleep in a car. CUT/

5b) Interior. Close-up shot of a string of rosary beads and a crucifix. A baby (Vincent) has just been born in hospital. Vincent's mother, Marie (Jayne Brook), has put her faith in God's hands rather than the local geneticist, deciding to conceive naturally. Notice that this complex scene sets the mood for everything that follows. Marie gives birth and we witness her joy. The baby cries. Voice-over: 'Ten fingers, ten toes was all that used to matter … not any more.' The baby's genetic profile is checked by a blood test immediately after birth. Notice that the puncture mark on the foot, resulting from the test, is obvious. The parents discover that the baby has a predicted life expectancy of 30.2 years, with a 99 per cent probability of a fatal heart condition. Quick cutting follows between the nurse and the anxious parents. Marie wants to name the baby 'Anton', after his father Antonio, however, Antonio (Elias Koteas) chooses 'Vincent Anton'. Marie holds her precious baby, defying the world, saying, 'I know he'll do something. You'll do something.' DISSOLVE/

5c) Exterior. Day. Vincent as a toddler in the garden, falls, then looks up at the sound of aeroplanes as they fly overhead. His mother rushes out. Voice-over: 'From an early age I came to think of myself as others thought me – chronically ill …' The 'golden light' has become faded. A 1950s 'retro' ambience is evident in the *mise en scène*. CUT/

5d) Exterior. Day. Vincent's little hand grasps the iron gates of a preschool he is unable to attend because of his inability to obtain insurance cover. The teacher (Elizabeth Dennehy) who has denied him access, expresses concern about his weak condition, saying, 'What if he fell?' CUT/

Segment 6: Brothers

6a) Interior. Day. Clinic. Vincent's parents decide to 'design' their second child in what has become known as the 'natural' way. The geneticist (Blair Underwood) discusses their designer baby. CUT/ Vincent as a toddler on the floor, playing with a molecular model. The doctor explains how he will automatically eradicate tendencies to baldness, obesity, drunkenness and violence. Vincent's mother interrupts: 'We didn't want …' His father concludes that they'd like to leave a few things to chance. The doctor gently explains that they want to give the baby the best possible chance, arguing that we have enough imperfections already built in. CUT/ Vincent's mother, looking at him playing on the floor. The doctor says, 'This child is still you – simply the best of you … You could conceive a thousand times naturally and never get such a result.' The doctor smiles kindly. DISSOLVE/ Lyrical MUSIC begins

6b) Interior. Day. Freeman house, 1950s 'retro' look. Antonio measures eight-year-old Anton who is already taller than the weedy and bespectacled 10-year-old Vincent. Voice-over: 'That's how my brother Anton came into the world – a son my father considered worthy of his name.' Their father embraces the taller son. Vincent erases his name from the measuring pole. CUT/

6c) Exterior. Day. Beach, golden light. Lyrical MUSIC. A voice-over moves the narrative a few years ahead. Anton and Vincent are blood brothers, but with very different blood. Vincent thinks he'll need more than a drop to get anywhere. He slices his thumb with a shell and hands it to Anton, who can't bring himself to mingle his blood with his brother's. Anton throws the shell down and runs into the sea. Their usual swimming challenge game 'Chicken' – about who can swim the farthest without turning back – ensues. Vincent's voice-over states: 'Of course, it was always me.' Notice the camera work – overhead shot of boys swimming from right to left of the screen. Vincent struggles. Anton calls, 'Come on, you coward.' Shot of Vincent floating, surrounded by seaweed. CUT/

6d) Exterior. Day. Parking lot. Vincent has set out the solar system in correct proportion, using balls and fruit for planets. The camera tracks from the 'sun', which fills the screen at the opening shot, along the ground, to find Anton and Vincent at the dwarf planet 'Pluto', where Vincent sets down a peach. Voice-over: 'Maybe it was a love of the planets ... giving me a dislike of this one.' Anton tries to eat the peach – Vincent prevents him from doing so. Anton sneers, 'I bet I could be an astronaut if I wanted.' CUT/

Segment 7: The turning point

7a) Interior. Day. Some years later in the Freeman home, dinnertime. The teenage Vincent is absorbed in a book on careers in science. Notice that he is not wearing glasses. Anton (Loren Dean) is eating. Their mother urges Vincent to be realistic with his heart condition. Their father picks up her signal to speak, when Vincent tells her that there is one chance in a hundred he's okay – and he'll take it. Antonio reiterates the negative view of Vincent's health, stating, 'The only way you'll see the inside of a spaceship is if you were cleaning it.' Close-up shot of Antonio from Vincent's point of view. CUT/

Voice-over: 'My father was right ... it didn't matter how much I lied on my resumé – my resumé was in my cells ... why should anybody waste all that money training me ... Of course, it's illegal to discriminate ... "genoism" it's called, but nobody takes the law seriously.'

7b) Interior. Day. Waiting room. Nerdy, spotty Vincent is waiting for his interview. He takes off his glasses and proceeds through a glass door to confront his interviewer – a stern-looking man (Clarence Graham). Voice-over enumerates how you can be checked genetically, however hard you try to cover up your defects, by samples taken from a door handle, handshake, even the saliva from your application envelope. Vincent is proffered a beaker for a urine test. Disheartened, he turns away. CUT/

7c) Key scene – The swim. Exterior. Day. Beach. Vincent and Anton are now young men, possessing different physical characteristics. Preceding another swimming competition, Anton asks Vincent, 'You're sure you want to do this? You know you're gonna lose.' MUSIC begins for the key moment. Voice-over: 'It was the last time we swam together.' Repeat camera shots recall an earlier swimming competition, which shows Vincent losing. This time, Vincent keeps up with Anton: 'Until finally, the impossible happened … it was the moment that made everything else possible.' Weedy Vincent saves exhausted Anton from drowning and brings him safely to shore. CUT/

7d) Key scene: Erasure of family identity. Interior. Night. Freeman house. Close-up shot of family photo. Vincent tears off one corner of the photo, erasing his face. Notice the deep focus shot of Anton entering the room, symbolically taking Vincent's place in the photo. Anton now appears as the only 'son' of the family. Anton watches Vincent, Vincent looks at Anton, both are wordless. Bespectacled Vincent (looking a bit like James Dean – this time a rebel with a cause) picks up his case and walks out into the deserted night street. DISSOLVE/

Segment 8: Vincent's resolve

Voice-over continues describing Vincent's life and comments on the new underclass: 'We now have discrimination down to a science.'

8a) A group of new cleaners arrives at Gattaca. Head cleaner, Caesar (Ernest Borgnine), greets them: 'Welcome to Gattaca, gentlemen.' Vincent is a cleaner, just as his father predicted. Notice that this is our first sight of Vincent, his head bowed, back to the camera, standing at the foot of the escalator. Vincent looks up and sees a rocket launch. He looks scruffy, punky and dim-witted, wearing glasses and chewing gum. Caesar calls out to him, 'Your majesty … dreaming of space?' CUT/

MUSIC continues over montage of Vincent's early experience of Gattaca.

8b) Exterior. Day. Golden dawn. Voice-over: 'I was never more certain of how far away I was from my goal when I was standing right beside it.' As a group of cleaners work on the glass roof, Vincent watches another launch. CUT/

8c) Interior. Night. Vincent is polishing the floor in the astronauts' workstation area. He steals some time to log on at a console and take a look. He gets up, waving, as Caesar appears in the distance. Shot shows his comic inability to handle the floor polisher effectively. CUT/

8d) Interior. Day. Caesar catches Vincent watching a launch whilst cleaning the windows. He says, 'When you clean the glass, Vincent, don't clean it too well ... you might get ideas.' Vincent replies, 'Yeah, but if the glass is clean it'll be easier for you to see me when I'm on the other side of it.' Notice the reflections of the Gattaca staff ascending the escalator behind Vincent. CUT/

8e) Interior. Gym. Night. Vincent finds and takes a heart monitor whilst cleaning. CUT/

8f) Interior. Night. Vincent is cleaning the entrance area. He pricks his finger on the blood test identity pad, which sets off the alarm. He realises that this is going to be a difficult problem to overcome. CUT/

8g) Interior. Night. Men's washroom. Vincent does strenuous exercises, using a book titled *Celestial Navigation* as a weight. He articulates the problem that even with the best-trained body, he needs the blood to go with it. Voice-over: 'I made up my mind to resort to more extreme measures.' CUT/

Segment 9: Vincent's ladder

9a) Interior. Vincent's home. Vincent negotiates with a black marketeer called German (Tony Shalhoub), who warns him that in the case of procuring a false identity, commitment is binding. Like the demon Mephistopheles' pact with Faustus, this bond, sealed in blood, is for Vincent's soul. German selects a test tube of blood from his wallet. Voice-over: 'For the genetically superior, success is easier to attain but by no means guaranteed. After all, there is no gene for fate ... When a member of the elite falls on hard times, their genetic identity becomes a valued commodity.' The voice-over serves as a bridge as Vincent is taken to meet his 'borrowed ladder' (a man whose genetic samples will be substituted for his own), who enables him to reach his goal. CUT/

9b) Exterior. Day. Jerome's apartment. Voice-over: 'One man's loss is another man's gain.' CUT/

9c) Interior. Day. We are led to anticipate an extraordinary person by German's description of Vincent's 'borrowed ladder' – super healthy, super intelligent, better than 20-20 vision, he'll live forever, could win a world war. He turns out to be a swimming star with a broken back. From weedy, crumpled Vincent's point of view, we witness Jerome (Jude Law) entering the room in a wheelchair – drunk, smoking, sullen and silent. German claims they look alike. Vincent disagrees. German is undeterred, declaring, 'With this guy's DNA tucked under your arm you could go anywhere ... Blood knows no nationality ... He's still a walking, talking, fully protected member of society.' Nobody really knows about Jerome's accident except that it happened abroad. Notice the empty bottles of alcohol lying around. In order to take on Jerome's identity, Vincent has just got to get him clean. Notice the spiral staircase, resembling the double-helix DNA. Vincent asks, 'Who lives up there?' This prompts Jerome's first words: 'Well, I certainly don't.' Notice the shadow on the wall, the duplicated self-image. CUT/

Segment 10: New identity

The MUSIC is upbeat. Voice-over: 'So began the process of becoming Jerome.' DISSOLVE into a montage of the process involved in changing Vincent's identity.

10a) Interior. German tests Vincent's eyes and corrects his myopia with contact lenses: myopia is one of the most obvious signs of a disadvantaged birth. Jerome watches, claiming that his eyes are prettier. CUT/

10b) Interior. Shot of a dentist at work as Jerome argues with German about money. CUT/

10c) Interior. Vincent is having his hair styled to replicate Jerome's hairstyle in his photo. The MUSIC stops as German tells Vincent there is a final difficulty – he must have leg-bone surgery to give him an extra two inches and bring his height to 6′1″. Jerome jokes that he is only 4′6″ in his wheelchair. Vincent refuses to have the surgery. Jerome taunts him: 'I thought you were serious.' Vincent replies, 'I am serious – I'm not doing that.' CUT/

10d) Close-up shot of a circular surgical saw, switched on. DISSOLVE/

10e) Interior. Day. Vincent lies flat on the floor, his legs in metal splints. Jerome is now satisfied that he is committed. 'Are you all right?' he asks. Vincent replies, 'Yeah ... Do you want to go dancing?' CUT/

Segment 11: Merging names

11a) Key scene. Interior. Day. Vincent, still immobilised, practises Jerome's signature. Jerome prepares samples at the bench. The relationship between the two is stressful, but is becoming stronger. Jerome's motivation for becoming a 'borrowed ladder' emerges from a conversation prompted by Vincent's comment that Jerome is a good name. 'It's my name,' Jerome says, 'What makes you think that you can be me?' Jerome shows Vincent his silver swimming medal. When Vincent makes light of it, he retorts, 'Are you blind as well, Vincent? What colour is it?' Jerome cannot bear the idea of coming second, one step down on the winner's podium. Jerome asks Vincent how he hopes to make it, if he, being born to succeed, was not able to. Vincent replies, 'I don't know exactly.' Jerome tells him that the signature needs more practice.

MUSIC begins. Voice-over about time to put it all to the test. CUT/

11b) Key scene. Exterior. Night. Long shot of Gattaca lit up. Jerome in his chair and Vincent on crutches look across the lake at the Gattaca building. Voice-over: 'Jerome had been engineered with every genetic advantage to get into Gattaca ... with everything except the desire to do so.' Jerome asks, 'Why do you want to be in there?' Vincent replies, 'I don't want to be in there – I want to be up there' (looking at the stars). Jerome asks, 'Why? What's up there?' Vincent replies, 'I don't know – that's what I want to find out, Jerome.' **Key moment:** Jerome says, 'Call me Eugene ... my middle name ... If you're going to be Jerome, you'd better get used to it.' Notice the *mise en scène* silhouettes of two men, watching the rocket launch. CUT/

11c) Interior. Day. The 'new' genetic hoax, Jerome/Vincent, is getting ready to go for his test and interview. The urine samples provided by Jerome/Eugene are all 'hot', contaminated with vodka – is the whole plan going to fail? CUT/ Jerome/Eugene drinking and working at his bench, suggesting that the test machine is reading faultily, because one sample is okay. Notice that now they look alike – smart, both dressed in suits. **Key moment:** Jerome/Vincent turns to Jerome/Eugene and says, 'Listen, it's not too late to back out. This is the last day you are going to be you and I am going to be me ... well?' Both are honourable men and allow the situation to continue. Jerome/Eugene's DNA will eventually benefit them both. Jerome/Eugene remains silent. In a medium close-up, Jerome/Vincent 'toasts' Jerome/Eugene with a urine sac and leaves. CUT/

11d) Interior. Day. Gattaca. Jerome/Vincent passes the urine test as VALID Jerome Morrow. Lamar says, 'Congratulations.' No further interview is required. Notice that suitable genes are all that matter. CUT/

11e) Interior. Day. Home. Jerome/Vincent descends the spiral staircase and tells Jerome/Eugene, situated in his chair at the foot of the stairs, 'I got it.' CUT/ Jerome/Eugene. Notice the pattern of the parquet flooring, radiating out from him like energy lines, sadly emphasising his immobility as an 'invalid' VALID. 'Of course you got it,' Jerome/Eugene replies. DISSOLVE/

Segment 12: Jerome/Vincent's routine begins

Interior. Day. Blue light. Gentle MUSIC. Voice-over: 'And that's the way it was ...'

12a) Jerome/Vincent uses the cleaning unit to ensure that he won't leave a trace of his INVALID self in the VALID world. Shot of Jerome/Eugene's superior genetic material samples of urine, blood and traces of hair and skin. 'While Eugene gave me a new identity,' Jerome/Vincent says, 'I paid the rent and kept him in the manner to which he had become accustomed.' Both men become smart Gattaca types, alpha personalities. CUT/

12b) Interior. Home. Jerome/Eugene is in his wheelchair, working carefully in the laboratory, checking samples. Jerome/Vincent's voice-over reflects on Jerome/Eugene's different burden. He wasn't an INVALID, 'utero' or 'faith birth', and didn't suffer the associated routine discrimination, but as a VALID, vitro, made man, he suffered the burden of perfection. CUT/

12c) Interior. Home. Jerome/Vincent checks the wardrobe that stores polythene-wrapped shirts and shoes. The voice-over states that Jerome/Vincent is now a detested figure in the new society – a 'borrowed ladder', a de-gene-erate. Jerome/Vincent throws his suit on the bed. The cleaner's label, marked 'confidentiality guaranteed', is exposed. Ask yourself why the dry cleaner would mark its product with such a label. What are the implications here? DISSOLVE/

END OF FLASHBACK, BACK TO MAIN NARRATIVE (left off at scene 6)

Segment 13: Crime scene and launch week

13a) Interior. Day. Gattaca. Jerome/Vincent is in the corner, looking at the murder scene. The voice-over reveals that only one of the mission directors ever came close to discovering his true identity and that they would have more success in exposing him in death than they ever did in life. This prompts us to ask why this would be so. Is it being suggested that Jerome/Vincent is a murder suspect? Jerome/Vincent walks up to the bleeding, battered head, turns and walks away. The camera pulls out to keep him in focus, then picks up Jerome/Vincent's eyelash on the window ledge. CUT/

13b) Interior. Gattaca. Investigation begins. Close-up of computer keyboard covered in blood. Detective Hugo (Alan Arkin) displays the wry humour of a canny 'gumshoe' detective: 'Well, I think we can rule out suicide.' This scene contains many noir elements, such as the raincoats and the hats. CUT/

13c) Interior. Workstation area. Investigation proceeds. Agents 'hoover', or vacuum, the area, collecting body samples. Detective Hugo tells Mission Director Josef that the investigation may take a while. CUT/ Jerome/Vincent watching impassively. Close-up shot of the detective vacuuming – collecting DNA evidence. CUT/ the Director asking Irene to help the detectives. She is reluctant to do so as she doesn't want to lose her place in line for a space mission. Jerome/Vincent asks the Director if the mission will be affected as there is a week-long window of opportunity and Jerome/Vincent is set to leave at the end of the week. The Director replies enigmatically: 'It hasn't stopped the planets turning, has it?' There is an exchange of small smiles between the two men. CUT/ extreme close-up moment: Jerome/Vincent's eyelash is vacuumed. CUT/

13d) Interior. Night. Home. Jerome/Eugene finds Jerome/Vincent drinking and asks, 'What happened?' Jerome/Vincent reports that he is going up at the end of the week. Jerome/Eugene replies, 'So soon?' Notice the significance of this scene – what is Jerome/Eugene planning to do when Jerome/Vincent goes? Jerome/Vincent reports that a Mission Director is dead – murdered, stating that there's nothing between them and ignition. Jerome/Eugene analyses the situation: 'There'll be an investigation ... a man was murdered ... there'll be hoovers everywhere.' Jerome/Vincent states that he can handle the J. Edgars (reference to J. Edgar Hoover, head of the FBI in the US in the 1940s–1960s). An atmosphere of high spirits ensues. Notice the decor, the classical painting behind Jerome/Eugene, symbolic of his culture and cultivated tastes. Jerome/Eugene declares, 'We have to get drunk immediately.' CUT/

Segment 14: Genetic success for Jerome/Vincent

Alternating sequence, cutting between men getting drunk at the Cavendish Club and Irene having Jerome/Vincent's DNA checked for his suitability as a future sexual partner.

14a) Interior. Night. Cavendish Club. Sophisticated 'retro' style, with black madam owner (Cynthia Martells), cool jazz. Jerome/Vincent and Jerome/ Eugene are getting drunk in style. CUT/

14b) Interior. Gattaca. Irene searches through Jerome/Vincent's workstation. In a drawer, she finds a hair in a comb. CUT/

14c) Interior. Public DNA-testing lab. A woman (Grace Sullivan) checks her boyfriend's DNA from a saliva swab taken from her mouth shortly after kissing him. Irene checks out Jerome/Vincent's DNA sequence. The result is 9.3, proving him to be quite a catch. CUT/

14d) Interior. Cavendish Club. Jerome/Eugene complains about the wine not being given enough time to breathe and tells Jerome/Vincent to remember that. Jerome/Vincent talks about being weightless, saying that it is the nearest thing to being in the womb. Jerome/Eugene says, 'I can't believe you pulled this off.' There is a strong bond between the two men now. What will Jerome/Eugene do – stuck in a room – while Jerome/ Vincent is away for a year? Jerome/Eugene avoids the question, asking, 'What's Titan like this time of year?' Silly casual conversation follows – or is it? Jerome/Vincent blows cigarette smoke into his glass to imitate the planet. Jerome/Vincent says to Jerome/Eugene, 'You should be going instead of me ... up there your legs wouldn't matter.' Jerome/Eugene graciously replies, 'I'm scared of heights.' A close-up shot brings the two men close together. CUT/

14e) Exterior. Night. Home. Long shot. While Jerome/Vincent plugs the electric car into the recharger socket, Jerome/Eugene vomits noisily, saying afterwards, 'Do you want this?' The idea of saving all useful bodily substances is taken to absurd lengths. CUT/

14f) Interior. Night. Home. Jerome/Vincent struggles upstairs with Jerome/Eugene to the bedroom. Both men are drunk. Jerome/Vincent says, 'Don't give me a hard time.' Jerome/Eugene confesses to Jerome/Vincent that he wasn't drunk when he stepped out in front of the car, indicating that his 'accident' was really a suicide attempt: 'I've never been more sober in my life ... couldn't even get that right, could I? If at first you don't succeed, try, try again. I'm proud of you, Vincent,' he says. Jerome/Vincent replies, 'You must be drunk to call me Vincent.' CUT/

Segment 15: Investigation proceeds

15a) Exterior. Night. Gattaca. Long shot, reminding us that a serious murder investigation is still going on.

15b) Interior. Night. Gattaca. Close-up of a bloody autopsy proceeding. Different items are scanned and tested, with 'VALID' flashing up on the screen. An eyelash is sucked into the machine, prompting an 'INVALID'. Vincent's old 'spotty youth' identity photo appears on the screen. The security chief (Vincent's brother Anton) looks up, asking, 'Who's this?' CUT/

Segment 16: An INVALID in Gattaca?

16a) Interior. Day. Home. A very hung-over Jerome/Eugene, in his wheelchair, does exercise equivalent to 20 minutes of heavy running for Jerome/Vincent's heart-monitor device. CUT/

16b) Interior. Day. Gattaca gymnasium. Irene, aware that her poor physical performance has been noted, is excused from any further exercise on the running machine. Jerome/Vincent begins his running, substituting the heart-monitor for the already-primed device. A superb, regular heartbeat appears on the screen. CUT/

MUSIC begins.

16c) Detective Hugo and Anton discuss the INVALID janitor – the prime murder suspect – and how to find him. Is Anton already covering up? Has he recognised his lost brother Vincent in the photo? Anton states that the INVALID is a very sick man with a 90 per cent chance of being dead and says that the security check has not traced any living relative for him. Notice that it is Anton who is the only living relative, as we find out later that Anton and Vincent's parents are dead. The old-style Detective agrees to run the investigation according to Anton's recommendations. Close-up shot of Anton's hand holding the eyelash in a vial. CUT/

16d) Interior. Gym. Jerome/Vincent is on the running machine. Lamar comments: 'Jerome, Jerome, the metronome ... could play piano by that heart.' There is an emotionless expression on Jerome/Vincent's face, signifying his steely determination. The Detective and Anton enter the gym. The Detective wants to post the INVALID's picture around. Shot of training astronauts. Anton watches and asks the Mission Director what it takes to be an astronaut. Recall Anton's boyhood boast: 'I bet I could be an astronaut if I wanted.' The Director describes the selection policy, making a pointed comment about how second-rate minds are capable of fulfilling the requirements of a law enforcement officer's position. Shot of Irene, resting, as the Director continues, describing how minor shortcomings can be overlooked. 'What Gattaca needs,' he says, 'is bodies with minds to match.' Is the Director aware that Jerome/Vincent is a fake? Is he suggesting that 'right' minds are free minds? Anton asks about those who exceed their potential. The Director replies that no-one exceeds their potential, because if they did it would mean Gattaca did not accurately gauge their potential in the first place. **Quick cutting sequence** begins – close-up shot of Jerome/Vincent running. His heart rate suddenly rises, indicating that the 20 minutes of recorded pacing has come to an end. The monitor reacts. The Doctor looks up, and the Director and Anton look around. Jerome/Vincent rips off the chest monitor, leaves the machine and casually exits the gym. CUT/

16e) Interior. Locker room. Jerome/Vincent collapses against the wire, struggling for breath, experiencing heart pain. CUT/

16f) Interior. Anton is walking. CUT/ Jerome/Vincent dressed in a suit, leaving. CUT/ Irene and Anton talking. CUT/ Interior. Jerome/Vincent, recovered, runs down the stairs. Caesar the janitor respectfully calls him Mr Morrow and offers to dispose of his used paper cup. Note that Caesar does not recognise Jerome/Vincent as the cleaner previously on his staff. CUT/

Notice how the fast cutting builds and maintains tension as Jerome/Vincent faces potential exposure.

Segment 17: Irene and Jerome/Vincent connect

Exterior. Day. Golden light. By the stark building, Irene stands watching a launch. She is joined by Jerome/Vincent, who says, 'See, I'm not the only one who looks up when there's a launch.' They discuss the murder of the Mission Director and remark that it was 'lucky', as he would have cancelled the Titan mission. Irene tells Jerome/Vincent that an INVALID's eyelash has been found. Is this perhaps what Anton has just told her? If so, why did he? Does he want Jerome/Vincent to know that he's been discovered? Does Irene now know, too? Irene confesses to Jerome/Vincent: 'I had you sequenced.' Notice that a man in a hat (a very noir image) walks beside the wall behind the couple in the two-shot. Why? Is this the moment of unmasking for Jerome/Vincent? It is established that Jerome/Vincent's identity remains secure as Irene apologises, stating, 'You're everything they say … and more.' This leads to Irene's confession of her failure as a potential astronaut, possessing an unacceptable risk of heart failure. She gives Jerome/Vincent a hair in order for him to prove her testimony by sequencing, and then says, 'If you're still interested, let me know.' Jerome/Vincent drops it. There is a close-up of the hair lying on the hard, arid ground, followed by Jerome/Vincent's gallant lie: 'I'm sorry, the wind caught it.' CUT/ black/

Segment 18: Jerome?

18a) Interior. Day. Camera tilts up, discovering the face of Jerome/Vincent reflected on the computer screen as he works. A shot from Jerome/Vincent's point of view reveals INVALID Vincent's face on the screen. Jerome/Vincent is shocked. CUT/ Shot of Irene's screen, where Jerome/Vincent's face also appears. She does not react. The Mission Director looms up behind Jerome/Vincent and points to the screen, asking, 'Jerome, is this the approach path we discussed?' Jerome/Vincent responds, 'Absolutely, Director.' The Director – whom one could assume is aware of Jerome/Vincent's identity – replies, 'Quite right, quite right.' CUT/

18b) Exterior. Night. Home. The sound of a car roaring home is heard. CUT/

18c) Key scene: Crisis point. Interior. Home. Jerome/Eugene is angrily talking to the hair colour supplier on the phone – they have sent the wrong shade. Jerome/Vincent descends the spiral staircase, telling Jerome/Eugene that they have to move, as he suspects the authorities will come to search the premises because his eyelash has been found. Notice how the camerawork draws the two men closer as the tension rises. Jerome/Eugene tries to calm Jerome/Vincent by stressing that they won't recognise his face. 'I don't recognise you,' he says. An argument between the two begins. Jerome/Vincent begins flushing samples down the toilet and Jerome/Eugene responds by grabbing the sample sachets, retorting, 'They're mine!' Jerome/Eugene continues his attempt to persuade Jerome/Vincent to be brave and continue by apparently ridiculing him and chasing him around the room in his wheelchair, declaring, 'I could have rented myself out to somebody with a spine! If I'd have known you'd go belly up on me at the last fucking gasp ... You can't quit on me now – I've put too much into this ... do you expect me to wheel in and finish the job myself?' **Key moment:** Jerome/Eugene's final point marks an important next step in the 'morphing' transition: 'You still don't understand, do you? When they look at you, they don't see you any more, they see me.' Jerome/Vincent hands back the blood sachet and Jerome/Eugene eases the tension with a gentle, campy, scolding joke: 'Keep your eyelashes on your lids, where they belong. How could you be so careless?' DISSOLVE, with MUSIC beginning as at beginning of film.

Segment 19: Jerome/Vincent prepares to attend recital

19a) Interior. Home. Blue light. Montage of detail shots. Jerome/Vincent thoroughly cleans himself in the shower, preparing for the evening out. CUT/

19b) Interior. Home. Jerome/Vincent descends the spiral staircase. Jerome/Eugene is having a drink. Jerome/Vincent must attend the evening's recital, as his absence would appear odd since everybody was expected to be there. Notice Jerome/Eugene's tone in response – indicating he understands that he is now nobody, no person, erased even, one could say, by Jerome/Vincent. Jerome/Eugene has to remind him to remove his glasses and wear contact lenses if he doesn't want to be recognised. CUT/

19c) Exterior. Night. Irene is in her car, waiting. She takes a pill, looks up and sees Jerome/Eugene looking down from the window. There is no recognition of him as 'Jerome'.

Segment 20: VALIDS and INVALIDS

Long alternating sequence begins. MUSIC over: Schubert *Impromptu*. Activities of Jerome/Vincent, Irene, Jerome/Eugene and Anton all crisscross as Detective Hugo's investigation continues.

20a) Interior. Recital hall. Irene and Jerome/Vincent sit and listen, their hands touching whilst the pianist plays.

20b) Exterior. Night. Streets. The police round up and test all INVALIDS, while Anton argues that a clever INVALID is not likely to be a derelict on the streets. He suggests they should sweep Gattaca again. CUT/

20c) Exterior. Night. A policeman (Dean Norris) tests Jerome/Eugene, who is outside in his wheelchair, watching the night sky, smoking. The policeman reads that he is a Gattaca Navigator and says that he is surprised there is no mention of him being a cripple. Jerome/Eugene enraged, turns on the policeman, retorting, 'What's your number? … How dare you question me? … I'm getting off this ball of dirt …' **Key moment:** Jerome/Eugene makes another move to full morphing – now he is identified as 'Jerome' completely. This marks a recovery of his 'real' identity and the appropriation of Jerome/Vincent's – the actual navigator who will be leaving the 'ball of dirt' the next day.

20d) Interior. Gattaca. Policemen comb the workstations again. Detective Hugo notices the cleaner Caesar and apprehends his bag of trash. (Look back at **16f** for the significance of this.)

20e) Interior. Recital hall. Aerial view of pianist, ornate floor. The recital ends to much applause and the pianist throws his gloves into the audience. Jerome/Vincent catches one and gives it to Irene. She puts it on, demonstrating that it has six fingers. Jerome/Vincent is shocked, particularly when the poster outside the hall shows the pianist covering his face with his 'freaky' 12 fingers. This is an ambiguous image. He seems to be hiding his face as if he feels ashamed or feels that his face doesn't matter – that his worth lies predominantly in his genetically designed hands. Unfazed, Irene explains coolly, 'That piece can only be played by 12.' Jerome/Vincent seems to express revulsion at the freakish nature of the pianist's hands. Does he feel freakish too or is his the 'healthy' response of a non-genetically manipulated human being? What does the pianist really feel about his hands?

Segment 21: 'Vincent' qualities protect 'Jerome'

21a) Exterior. Night. Irene, with Jerome/Vincent as passenger, drives through the 'mean streets'. In the tunnel there is a roadblock, where police are testing everyone's identity. Jerome/Vincent casually flicks out his contact lenses. The camera shows his myopic point of view. Notice that the policeman checks his eyes with a fluoroscope and they test okay. Jerome/Vincent avoids having a saliva test. His blood test reads VALID. Through the roadblock, Irene says she wants to show him something. Shot of Jerome/Vincent's myopic point of view. CUT/

Rapid cutting sequence begins.

21b) Irene parks the car and runs across the busy road. She waits for Jerome/Vincent to follow her. CUT/ Jerome/Vincent's myopic point of view. Blurred lights are hurtling towards him. Jerome/Vincent must simply dare to risk crossing because he can't see properly. Jerome/Vincent joins Irene who appears puzzled. They hurry along. CUT/

21c) Solar farm, panels catching the sun's rays at dawn. Shot of Jerome/Vincent's point of view, depicting a blurred impression as he looks across the panels with Irene. She remarks, 'Your eyes look different,' as they walk between the rows of panels in the golden dawn. Jerome/Vincent replies, 'It must be the light.' CUT/

Segment 22: Anton swimming

Interior. Blue water. Anton's swimming pool. Anton is practising hard. The memory of his defeat by the puny Vincent as a child obviously still rankles him. His watch-phone rings. CUT/

Segment 23: Blood test

23a) Interior. Gattaca. Hugo reveals a genetic match with the INVALID from a paper cup. It is revealed that their suspect murderer must be using a 'borrowed ladder' for his Gattaca identity. Therefore, they conclude that the testing of blood from a vein is the only reliable identity test available for use in the investigation. CUT/

23b) Interior. Day. Gattaca. All Gattaca staff are lining up for a blood test. Lamar appears to facilitate Jerome/Vincent's faked 'ouch', which enables him, with the policeman looking, to swap the test tube of blood with Jerome/Eugene's sample, which procures a VALID reading. CUT/

23c) Interior. Day. Jerome/Vincent and Irene meet briefly after the blood test. CUT/

23d) Interior. Day. The testing is finished. No INVALIDS have been detected. Detective Hugo, standing with Anton and the Mission Director, knows something is wrong and wants to re-test all the staff. The Director asserts that they cannot delay the launch – they must take the one-week-in-70-years window of opportunity. The Director deflects the Detective's implication that he might have anything to do with the murder, declaring that if they check his profile, they will find not a violent bone in his body. CUT/

MUSIC. Jazz as bridge, linking to the next scene.

Segment 24: Two days to launch

24a) Interior. Night. Home. Jerome/Eugene is doing wheelies around the bench, preparing lots of blood and urine samples. His actions appear purposeful and communicate a sense of urgency. CUT/

24b) Interior. Night. Cavendish Club. Jerome/Vincent takes Irene (notice that her hair is down) to dinner. At the table, she takes her pills, saying, 'I'm luckier than most.' Jerome/Vincent invites her to dance, which is a serious reprise of the mock-joking with Jerome/Eugene in an earlier scene. A romantic atmosphere envelops the couple as they contemplate a year of separation. Detective Hugo, Anton and the police raid the club. People start to scatter. Notice that this society is not as well-controlled as its controllers would like to think. Do the scattering crowds indicate that there are many secrets being hidden from the police? CUT/

24c) Exterior. Night. Alley behind the club. Irene is pushed out through the back door by Jerome/Vincent. She leaves her pillbox behind and Anton picks it up. A policeman tries to stop Jerome/Vincent and his violent survival response shocks Irene. They run along the alley. She collapses due to her weak heart, so they shelter in a doorway. As Detective Hugo swabs the mouth of the beaten cop for DNA clues, Anton looks along the street, calling, 'Vincent!' CUT/ Irene, mouthing, 'Who's Vincent?' They don't speak but kiss instead. DISSOLVE with MUSIC to the next scene.

Segment 25: Irene and Jerome/Vincent

25a) Interior. Night. Irene's beach house. Short montage of lovemaking, waves breaking on shore through window, superimposed images.

25b) Interior/Exterior. Dawn. Jerome/Vincent wakes up beside Irene and sees a strand of hair on the pillow. He realises that he must clean himself as usual for work. On the beach, he scrubs his body with sand, shells and sea water. This is risky, as it is not as thorough as his usual cleansing routine. Irene asks about the scars on Jerome/Vincent's legs, stating she knows that he is somehow connected with the Director's death. CUT/

Segment 26: Anton's pursuit – the day before the launch

26a) Interior. Morning. Gattaca. Anton switches between the computer images of VALID Jerome and INVALID Vincent. Detective Hugo appears and asks about the man. Anton declares that he's nobody and switches off the monitor. At this point, we must ask ourselves whether Anton is protecting Vincent or whether he is enraged that the INVALID Vincent has beaten him yet again. CUT/

26b) Interior. Day. Anton confronts the Mission Director, who replies audibly that Jerome/Vincent is one of the best. Irene overhears, turns and leaves – Anton notices. CUT/

26c) Interior. Day. At the blood test entrance point, Irene gives Jerome/Vincent a warning, saying, 'Jerome, you don't look well. Why don't you go home?' He takes the hint, turns and walks out. CUT/

26d) Interior. Day. Anton stops Irene, stating that he needs to meet Jerome/Vincent. She makes an excuse about an astronaut's understandable nausea the day before a mission launch. However, she knows where he lives and must eventually show Anton. CUT/

Cutting speeds up from now on – viewer tension rises

MUSIC begins

Segment 27: Hugo finds the culprit

Interior. Day. Gattaca morgue. Detective Hugo looks at a dead body – analyses unknown. The liquid content of a phial is placed beside the corpse. The results appear on the screen, just out of the viewer's field of vision. Who is the culprit? CUT/

Segment 28: Who is 'Jerome'?

Rapid alternating sequence.

28a) Interior. Gattaca. Upstairs, looking down the escalator, Jerome/Vincent tries to make a phone call to Jerome/Eugene. CUT/

28b) Interior. Home. Downstairs. Jerome/Eugene sits at the bench, urgently preparing body samples, irritated by the interruption of the ringing phone. CUT/

a) Interior. Gattaca. Jerome/Vincent persists in trying to call Jerome/Eugene, muttering, 'Come on.' CUT/

28c) Interior. Gattaca. At the foot of the escalator, Anton gives Irene her pillbox, stating, 'You don't know who he is, do you, Irene?' Notice that the entrance at the foot of the escalator is where Jerome/Vincent started to penetrate Gattaca in scene 12a.

a) Interior. Gattaca. Jerome/Vincent is still impatiently trying to call Jerome/Eugene. CUT/

b) Interior. Home. Jerome/Eugene mutters angrily at the ringing phone, consciously ignoring it. CUT/

28d) Exterior. Gattaca. Anton's car draws away from the escalator entrance. CUT/

a) Interior. Gattaca. Jerome/Vincent is still desperately phoning Jerome/Eugene. CUT/

b) Interior. Home. Jerome/Eugene answers the phone at last. CUT/

a) Interior. Gattaca. Jerome/Vincent warns Jerome/Eugene, pleading with him: 'I need you to be yourself for today, okay?' CUT/

b) Interior. Home. Jerome/Eugene looks up the spiral staircase, replying, 'I was never very good at it, remember?' Does he mean that he was never very good at being himself or at swimming? Notice that this is an interesting comment for him to make. CUT/

a) Interior. Gattaca. Jerome/Vincent says, 'The investigators are coming by.' CUT/

b) Interior. Home. Jerome/Eugene asks, 'How long have I got?' Music important here.

b) Jerome/Eugene flings himself out of his wheelchair and begins to haul himself up the stairs, spiralling around the helix. CUT/

c) Exterior. Anton's car arrives. Anton and Irene walk to the door and ring the bell several times. ALTERNATING WITH/

b) Key scene: Jerome/Eugene's champion swim. Interior shots of Jerome/Eugene hauling himself upstairs, reaching towards the intercom button. He 'swims' up the helix stairs, an athletic marvel, demonstrating the strength of his swimmer's arms.

Segment 29: Valid test

29a) Alternation sequence ends with Jerome/Eugene arranging himself upstairs in a 'casual' sitting position, facing the apartment entrance door. The shot depicts his point of view as Anton and Irene enter. They are puzzled to see him and not Jerome/Vincent. Jerome/Eugene establishes a 'relationship' with Irene to allay Anton's suspicions. He greets her, saying, 'Hello, sweetheart,' and asks her for a kiss. She plays along. Anton takes blood from his vein and the test reads VALID. Jerome/Eugene appears puzzled, asking, 'Who were you expecting?' Silent with cold rage, Anton looks around, then starts to descend the spiral staircase. CUT/

29b) Interior. Downstairs (Jerome/Eugene's territory). As Anton descends towards the laboratory area, Jerome/Vincent is seen in the foreground, hiding behind a pillar. Anton is informed that they have their man in custody. He leaves quickly. CUT/

a) Interior. Upstairs. Irene is perplexed. Does she fear that the man arrested is her Jerome/Vincent? As she and Jerome/Eugene stare at each other, Jerome/Vincent appears, climbing the stairs. Notice the beautiful framing of the two-shot for this moment of revelation for Irene. Jerome/Vincent asks, 'How are you, Jerome?' Jerome/Eugene appears relieved. With a small smile, he replies, 'Not bad, Jerome.' Jerome/Vincent asks, 'How the hell did you get up here?' Jerome/Eugene jokes, 'Oh, I could always walk – I've been faking it.' Irene looks, smiles slightly, turns and leaves. CUT/

Segment 30: Jerome/Vincent and Irene

Exterior. Apartment. Jerome/Vincent catches up with Irene as she storms away. In this **key scene**, he confronts her with the truth of his 'monstrosity'. He also confronts her with her own self-defeating sense of being ill, defective and disabled because of her heart condition. Elaborating further on his own weakness, he concludes that it *is* possible to triumph over genetic determinism. CUT/

Segment 31: Murder solved

31a) Exterior. Gattaca. Anton's car arrives. CUT/

31b) Interior. Gattaca. Anton finds the Mission Director and Detective Hugo together. It has been found that the Director's spit has been detected in the murdered man's eye, proving that the INVALID had nothing to do with the murder. Anton is stunned. It is decided that the launch will go ahead the next day anyway, with Jerome/Vincent navigating. CUT/

Segment 32: DNA bond

Interior. Home. The sound of Jerome/Vincent's footsteps are heard carrying Jerome/Eugene down the spiral staircase. Jerome/Eugene says, 'I think she likes us.' Jerome/Vincent replies, 'She'll get used to it.' Being aware of who Anton is, Jerome/Vincent knows he has to meet with him. CUT/

Segment 33: Are we brothers?

33a) Interior. Gattaca. Anton is at Jerome/Vincent's keyboard. The sound of footsteps is heard. Jerome/Vincent's point of view is depicted as the camera tracks towards his workstation. Anton knows without looking that it is his brother approaching: 'Vincent?' The brothers look at each other, shot-reverse-shot. Jerome/Vincent asks, 'Are we brothers?' **Crisis point:** Anton is enraged at the way Vincent dares to exceed the boundary of his DNA 'capacity'. Remember that Anton still has difficulty accepting that he ever needed 'weakling' Vincent's help in the swimming competition (see drowning episode, scene **7c**). CUT/

33b) Key scene. Exterior. Night. At the sea's edge, Anton and Vincent, dressed in suits, begin to get undressed. They run naked into the sea. The MUSIC is important here. Shots recall the earlier swimming contest, but reversed this time – it's a return to the childhood contest, providing closure to the experience. Anton panics: 'Vincent? Where's the shore? We're too far out.' Vincent asks, 'You want to quit?' Anton then demands to know Vincent's secret – how he managed to defeat his superior DNA.

'This is how I did it, Anton,' Vincent says, 'I never saved anything for the swim back.' Vincent's human will, daring and his courage to live and achieve ambitious goals are asserted as the key factors in this scene. Anton turns, swims back, sinks and is rescued again by Vincent. They drift back, Vincent looking up at the stars. The MUSIC ends, followed by a FADE TO BLACK/

Segment 34: Launch day

34a) Key scene: Lovers. FADE IN/ Exterior. Dawn. Silence. Irene has slept in the car. She wakes and sees Jerome/Vincent in the wing mirror, resting, dishevelled. Irene says: 'You couldn't see, could you? ... You crossed anyway.' Jerome/Vincent gives her a strand of his hair, saying, 'If you're still interested, let me know.' Notice that this is an echo of segment 17. Irene lets the strand of hair go, saying, 'Sorry, the wind caught it.' The MUSIC begins. DISSOLVE/

34b) Interior. Morning. The couple are peacefully asleep in bed. DISSOLVE/

34c) Key scene: Brotherly Love. Interior. Morning. Home. Jerome/Vincent returns to find the laboratory cleaned and packed up. Jerome/Eugene emerges from the walk-in refrigerator, saying, 'You're flying today, aren't you? Look at what a mess you're in! Your samples are ready.' Although Jerome/Vincent claims he won't need samples where he's going, Jerome/Eugene has thought ahead: 'You might when you get back ... enough for two lifetimes.' Jerome/Vincent asks, 'Why have you done all this?' Jerome/Eugene replies, 'So Jerome will always be here when you need him.' 'Where are you going?' asks Jerome/Vincent. 'I'm going travelling, too,' replies Jerome/Eugene. Notice how the shots are framed. The close-up shot of Jerome/Eugene looking up against a blue background and the medium close-up shot of Jerome/Vincent looking down against a split blue and golden background provide a cue for the imminent conclusion of their relationship. Jerome/Vincent remarks, 'I don't know how to thank you.' Jerome/Eugene replies, 'No, no, no, I got the better end of the deal. I only lent you my body. You lent me your dream.' Jerome/Eugene hands Jerome/Vincent an envelope, asking him not to open it until he's up there. CUT/

Segment 35: Vincent again

35a) Interior. Gattaca. Day. An overhead shot shows Jerome/Vincent, dressed in a smart suit, walking along an echoing, lit pathway, joining the other astronauts. Notice the mixed race, gender and age groups of the astronauts. Jerome/Vincent strikes a problem. A new policy requiring a final urine sample prior to boarding has been introduced. Jerome/Vincent, unprepared, experiences difficulty in providing a specimen. The laconic Lamar suggests this may be due to nerves. Jerome/Vincent assumes at this point that he'll be revealed as an INVALID and that his quest will be over. Lamar then says, 'I never did tell you about my son, did I? Big fan of yours ...' Jerome/Vincent says, 'Just remember that I was as good as any and better than most.' The doctor continues to speak: 'He wants to apply here. Unfortunately, my son's not as good as they promised ... but then who knows what he could do.' Jerome/Vincent's urine sample registers as INVALID as he had anticipated. Jerome/Vincent glances at Lamar, who calmly says, 'For future reference – right-handed men don't hold it with their left, just one of those things.' Jerome/Vincent presses a button on the screen in order to erase his image and the screen replaces his identity with VALID Jerome's. Notice the details of the status cards. The INVALID card is marked with a cross, similar in design to a rosary crucifix and the VALID card is marked with the figure '8', suggestive of the infinity sign and the DNA spiral helix. As Jerome/Vincent walks towards the launch bay entrance, the doctor wishes him well by his name, Vincent. CUT/

Segment 36: Going travelling

Alternation sequence begins. MUSIC – significant. Cutting between Jerome/Vincent in the rocket and Jerome/Eugene in the apartment.

36a) Interior. Gattaca. Jerome/Vincent walks down the lit passage (notice that the left one is open and the right one is closed at the entrance). He enters the rocket. This scene is symbolic of his rebirth.

36b) Interior. Home. Jerome/Eugene hauls himself into the cleaning unit. Behind him we can see the foot of the spiral staircase. He hangs his silver swimming medal around his neck and presses the button to start up the motor of the incinerator.

a) Exterior. Rocket blasts off.

b) Interior. Home. Jerome/Eugene's body is consumed in the incinerator. A close-up shot of his medal is followed by an extreme close-up of two men swimming together.

a) Interior. Rocket. A close-up shot of Jerome/Vincent shows him opening Jerome/Eugene's card containing a lock of his hair, enabling his DNA to go travelling into space with Jerome/Vincent. Jerome/Vincent's voice-over concludes: 'For someone who was never meant to stay on Earth, I'm suddenly having a hard time leaving it ... all once part of the stars ... maybe I'm not leaving, maybe I'm going home.' From Jerome/Vincent's point of view, the camera slowly zooms out through the porthole and the screen is filled with stars. SILENCE, hold view, then FADE TO BLACK.

MUSIC again for CREDITS. Watch to the end: you'll see a CUT/ blue, with an amplified rumbling sound and two fingernail parings crashing to the ground, as in the opening scene. Is your response to this visual information different now?

CHARACTERS & RELATIONSHIPS

Vincent

Key quotes

'My resumé was in my cells.' (**7a**)

'... the impossible happened. It was the moment that made everything else possible.' (**7c**)

'I was never more certain of how far away I was from my goal when I was standing right beside it.' (**8b**)

'For someone who was never meant to stay on Earth, I'm suddenly having a hard time leaving it ... maybe I'm not leaving, maybe I'm going home.' (**36a**)

Taking up the narrative in present time, the camera scrutinises details of Vincent's body as he prepares for another working day at Gattaca. INVALID Vincent is preoccupied with leaving a VALID genetic trail. His meticulous cleaning and careful planting of Jerome/Eugene's substitute DNA at his workstation require constant attention because Gattaca monitors its workers through random substance tests. If he is to achieve his dream of going into space in a week's time, he must continue to pass successfully as 'Jerome'. A murder investigation at Gattaca is suddenly complicating his careful routines.

Director Josef, Lamar and Irene all comment on Jerome/Vincent's apparently cool efficiency. As Vincent takes us back to his birth, childhood and entry into Gattaca (flashback segments **5–12**) we begin to understand how much determination it has taken to get him to the threshold of his dream. Underneath the calm surface is another ongoing reality of intense physical, emotional and intellectual struggle.

The flashback is significant because it demonstrates how Vincent's early interest in science (**6a, 6d, 7a**) has helped him overcome the drawbacks of his childhood. Resisting the psychologically negative messages from his parents and VALID brother Anton, he learns first how to deal with failure, of being thought ill (**5c, 7a**), being shut out of school (**5d**), repeatedly losing the swimming challenge (**6c**) and flunking job interviews (**7b**). At the point where he could be crushed, he unexpectedly beats Anton in the swimming challenge (**7c**), leaves home and gets to Gattaca. Almost defeated again, Vincent decides to take charge of his own future by investing in a 'borrowed ladder' and, as VALID 'Jerome', he is accepted as a trainee astronaut.

Vincent's emotional personality is enriched by his association with Jerome/Eugene and Irene, both of whom love him. He is also helped by Lamar and Director Josef, who may both be protecting him for their own reasons. All of them want to see Vincent achieve his dream. Does the film indicate that Vincent realises how important their support is? Remember, it isn't just Jerome/Eugene's DNA that gets Vincent through. It's a combination of his courageous personality and the actions of his supporters, too.

Anton

Key quotes

'Come on, you coward!' (**6c**)

'I bet I could be an astronaut if I wanted.' (**6d**)

Although he was a genetically designed VALID baby (**6a**), Anton lacks the intelligence, driving will and courage of his apparently weaker INVALID brother. In childhood he sneers at the planetary model (**6d**), dismissing Vincent's aspirations with casual arrogance. He also taunts his sibling with cowardice in their swimming contest (**6c**). The humiliation he feels when Vincent finally beats him and then has to save him from drowning (**7c**) cuts deep: as an adult, Anton still practises swimming obsessively without pleasure at home (**22**).

Anton's pride in his position as security chief is again challenged by INVALID Vincent's invasion of Gattaca. Anton appears to have fallen down on his job. At first he cannot believe his brother is still alive, against the odds, let alone a member of the Gattaca elite. In response to Detective Hugo's question about the photograph onscreen (**26a**), Anton answers, 'He's nobody,' as he shuts off the monitor. Is he protecting his brother? Does he think Vincent might be the murderer? Or is this another challenge to defend his VALID ego status by finally outsmarting his renegade brother?

After enduring Director Josef's pointed comment on second-rate minds capable of being law enforcement officers but not astronauts (**16d**), Anton's ego is bruised again. He looks tense and angry when his raid on the Cavendish Club fails to catch Vincent (**24c**), and again when he confronts Jerome/Eugene at home for the second blood test (**29a, b**). Even when he finds out that the INVALID had nothing to do with the murder (**31b**), Anton knows that another issue remains to be settled. In the last swim, he is again beaten and rescued by Vincent. What happens to him afterwards remains unknown.

The core motivation for Anton is to prove (to himself and to Vincent) that his genetically engineered DNA is superior to his brother's. His parents brought him up to believe he was the family champion – and he failed. His job is to protect Gattaca's genetic purity – and he fails. Vincent's success undermines everything that Anton has been led to accept as the social norm. Driven by rivalry and perplexed by Vincent's success, he ends up angry and embittered because his belief in the VALID/INVALID genetic divide has been undermined. Is the viewer encouraged to have any sympathy for Anton?

Vincent & Anton

Key quotes

'You sure you want to do this? You know you're gonna lose.' (**7c**)

'Are we brothers?' (**33a**)

'This is how I did it, Anton – I never saved anything for the swim back.' (**33b**)

The brothers have nothing in common as personalities, even though they share the same family blood. While Anton is a combative child, Vincent is more eager to be friendly. This is illustrated in the beach scene (**6c**), where Anton flinches and refuses the offer to become 'blood brothers' when Vincent deliberately cuts his hand before a swim. Does he throw down the seashell because he fears pain or because he is repelled by the thought of contamination by INVALID blood? Vincent's final challenge, 'Are we brothers?' can only be answered by Anton with another challenge – to repeat the swim. To Anton, Vincent's wholeheartedly courageous tactic of never saving anything for the swim back is too frightening and dangerous to consider.

Jerome

Key quotes

'What makes you think that you can be me?' (**11a**)

'We have to get drunk immediately!' (**13d**)

'What's Titan like this time of year?' (**14d**)

'I'm going travelling, too.' (**34c**)

When we first see Jerome, the swimming champion with the broken back, he looks the reverse of the heroic VALID description German has just given Vincent (**9c**). He is crippled in spirit as well as body, an aggressive, alcoholic, bitter man. Jerome's perfect DNA will be Vincent's 'borrowed ladder' to enter Gattaca, but somehow it hasn't ensured success for Jerome himself. Like Anton, Jerome has experienced the humiliation of being a VALID who has failed to benefit from his supposedly superior genetic makeup. He reveals to Vincent that winning a silver Olympic medal for swimming (**11a**) was so crushing that he attempted suicide – and he couldn't even get that right (**14f**).

While Jerome's first name becomes identified with the samples in the fridge for Vincent's use, his second name, 'Eugene' (well born), signals another identity – highly intelligent, cultivated, animated and generous. His death as Vincent leaves Earth is not a suicidal act Jerome gets right at last but, rather, a final mark of Eugene's generosity, leaving his remaining genetic trace to Vincent alone. A lock of Eugene's hair goes with Vincent on the Titan mission.

Vincent & Jerome

Key quotes

'One man's loss is another man's gain.' (**9b**)

Jerome: 'Are you all right?' Vincent: 'Yeah, Do you want to go dancing?' (**10e**)

'Listen, it's not too late to back out. This is the last day you are going to be you and I am going to be me.' (**11c**)

'You should be going instead of me. Up there your legs wouldn't matter.' (**14d**)

'I'm proud of you, Vincent.' (**14f**)

'You can't quit on me now – I've put too much into this.' (**18c**)

'You still don't understand, do you? When they look at you, they don't see you any more, they see me.' (**18c**)

'How are you, Jerome? ... Not bad, Jerome.' (**29a**)

'I think she likes us.' (**32**)

'I got the better end of the deal. I only lent you my body. You lent me your dream.' (**34c**)

Vincent starts out with the attitude that he is simply buying crippled Jerome's DNA as his 'borrowed ladder', but very soon a friendship grows between them. Finally, they exemplify the idea that 'brotherhood' bound by respect is mutually supportive and enriching, and has little to do with conventional siblings.

Vincent and Jerome together create the *Gattaca* hero 'Jerome', an identity that will help them both to go travelling. Notice that 'Jerome' sounds very like '**genome**', with slight errors in spelling. Perhaps this is a reminder of the unknown but significant 'chance' factors in genetic manipulation.

The short but intense relationship between Vincent and Jerome is significant for several reasons:

- It nurtures Jerome's recovery to the point where he not only defends but also shares Vincent's dream. This is initiated as the two men look at Gattaca and the night sky (**11b**), developed when Vincent describes Titan to Jerome (**14d**) and defended in his retort to the insulting cop who calls him a cripple (**20c**). Saying goodbye, Jerome thanks Vincent for lending him his dream (**34c**).
- Vincent learns from Jerome's initially hostile mocking attitude to stimulate his resolve and pay attention to details. Jerome's genuine anger pushes him through an almost catastrophic moment of panic as the criminal investigation closes in (**18c**).
- Vincent and Jerome's co-operative behaviour and verbal humour defeat Gattaca culture's isolating, DNA-obsessed, joyless approach to life.
- Jerome is motivated to complete a champion 'swim' up the spiral staircase to protect Vincent (**28b**), erasing the shame of his silver-medal attempt. Even Vincent is amazed by the result. Both men share the same capacity to commit themselves courageously.

Irene & Vincent

Key quotes

'If you're going to pretend like you don't care, don't look up.' (**4c**)

'See, I'm not the only one who looks up when there's a launch.' (**17**)

'Jerome, I had you sequenced.' (**17**)

'If you're still interested, let me know.' (**17**)

'Jerome, you don't look well. Why don't you go home?' (**26c**)

'You don't know who he is, do you, Irene?' (**28c**)

'You couldn't see, could you? ... You crossed anyway.' (**34a**)

Irene's cool exterior masks another passionate but disappointed VALID who has accepted that her debilitating heart defect will hold her back from achieving her dreams. We suspect at first that she is hostile to Vincent for getting his space flight first (**4c**): Director Josef responds sharply when she reveals her anxiety about losing her place if she takes time to help the murder investigation (**13c**). When we next see her checking around Vincent's workstation, it appears that she might be hoping to find incriminating evidence against him (**14b**). In fact, she's looking for some of his DNA to sequence and later discovers that she's made 'quite a catch' (**14c**). She signals her interest in Vincent by inviting him to have her DNA sequenced, too (**17**).

Because he lets the hair she gives him blow away, she finally tells him about her defective heart. Vincent says nothing yet about his similar flaw (a 99 per cent probability of a fatal heart condition). The scenes in the gym show that their hearts are similarly strained (**16**). As their relationship deepens, Irene is still puzzled by Vincent's eyes (**21c**) and the scars on his legs (**25b**) but she finally has to confront the true extent of Vincent's deception (**29a**) after she has gone along with the deception practised on Anton by Jerome.

Irene's character in the film is not developed much beyond her role as lover and helper to the rocket-navigator hero. While she may listen to his message that it's only herself that's holding her back from achievement (**30**), the film shows that she, unlike Vincent, has not been nurtured by

Director Josef and her dream to fly will not be endorsed by Gattaca. Her angry, unsure response to Vincent's genetic fraud (**30**) suggests a sudden recognition of ethical problems VALIDS would hardly ever expect to encounter. Ask yourself whether, as a VALID, you would/would not support a fraudulent INVALID. Why/why not?

Secondary characters

These characters are not developed but they play a significant part in Vincent's path to success at Gattaca, while illustrating a range of subversive attitudes to genetic elitism.

Lamar

Key quotes

'Have I ever told you about my son?' (**4b**)

'Unfortunately, my son's not as good as they promised ... but then, who knows what he could do.' (**35a**)

'For future reference – right-handed men don't hold it with their left, just one of those things.' (**35a**)

Lamar's laconic comment on Vincent's beautiful piece of equipment during his routine urine test (**4b**) – actually referring to Vincent's own non-genetically engineered penis – is motivated by more than good-natured envy. He appears to notice something unusual at the first test (**11d**), but it is only when a heartbroken Vincent is convinced that he will fail his last test (**35a**) without Jerome's sample that Lamar reveals the simple anatomical detail that gives Vincent away as an imposter from the beginning. Each time Lamar comments on Vincent's penis, he may be trying to warn him about betraying his INVALID status as a left-hander. Vincent himself tells us, 'Nobody orders southpaws any more' (**11a**).

Why does Lamar let Vincent pass as Jerome? As Vincent says wearily, 'Just remember that I was as good as any and better than most,' Lamar begins to tell the full story of his son, another less-than-perfect VALID, who is unlikely to be allowed to train at Gattaca, but then who knows what he might do given Vincent's example. Lamar ensures that Vincent's sample registers as VALID and finally calls him by his own name.

Director Josef

Key quotes

'It's right that someone like you is taking us to Titan.' (**4a**)

'It hasn't stopped the planets turning, has it?' (**13c**)

'No-one exceeds potential – if he did it would mean we did not accurately gauge his potential in the first place.' (**16d**)

'There's not a violent bone in my body.' (**23d**)

Does Director Josef know that Vincent is not who he claims to be? If the Director who was killed had nearly cracked Vincent's identity, Josef might have done so, too. When Vincent says he's heard talk of the mission being delayed, Josef replies, 'You shouldn't listen to talk ...' (**4a**). Josef reacts calmly to the murder (**13c**) and is finally revealed by DNA evidence as the killer of the Director who posed a threat to Vincent (**31b**).

All his comments may be read as coded approval of Vincent playing Jerome. He recognises an essential combination of intelligence and vision in the young man. Because he may be undermining Gattaca's genetic elitism to protect Vincent, you could think of Josef as a non-biological but highly effective father figure.

Josef calmly warns off Anton in the gym (**16d**) and outfaces Detective Hugo in the conversation about violence (**23d**), but the fact that he, as a high-level VALID, has still been capable of a very violent homicide, reinforces a view taken in the film that there is no correlation between good-quality genes and rationality. If Josef has killed to protect Vincent and thereby improve the chances of mission success, is his act in any way justifiable?

Detective Hugo

Key quotes

'Well, I think we can rule out suicide.' (**13b**)

This wry humour from a 'hard-boiled' cop belies Hugo's real intelligence. His approach to the crime scene is methodical and thorough. He gets the job done by sifting available evidence and accounting for all DNA traces.

Unlike Anton (who assumes that the eyelash belongs to an INVALID culprit), Hugo is open to the possibility that the criminal may be a VALID.

German

Key quotes

'The commitment is binding.' (**9a**)

'Blood knows no nationality.' (**9c**)

As a genetic broker working outside the law, German subverts the state itself at a basic level by trading in VALID identities. Is his activity criminal? Unlike Mephistopheles, who cheated Faustus while pretending to introduce him to unlimited knowledge in return for his soul, German's professional skills transform Vincent physically so that he can truly benefit from the transaction. German's name itself refers to genetics as well as to the Faustus story: the terms 'germen', 'germ' and 'germ-line' all refer to DNA 'seed'.

Minor characters

Antonio

Key quotes

'The only way you'll see the inside of a spaceship is if you were cleaning it.' (**7a**)

Antonio's disappointment at hearing newborn Vincent's genetic profile is obvious. His natural father's discouraging comment may actually give Vincent the idea for a legitimate way to get into Gattaca. Vincent knows his brother is the son his father considered worthy of his name (**6b**). What qualities in Anton do we see Antonio rewarding?

Marie

Key quotes

'I know he'll do something. You'll do something.' (**5b**)

Vincent has a hopeful, loving, protective mother, but her anxieties for his health reinforce her husband's disappointed, negative outlook for the boy. The film may be suggesting that her faith has been inspirational because it has given him his capacity to dream, to wonder about the cosmos.

Geneticist

Key quotes

'This child is still you – simply the best of you.' (**6a**)

'You could conceive a thousand times naturally and never get such a result' (**6a**)

The geneticist at the clinic puts the positive eugenics argument to Antonio and Maria, that genetic engineering is for the family's good, stating that it is simply using the best of what they are to produce a baby with the best possible genetic makeup. The doctor smiles kindly at INVALID toddler Vincent, who plays happily on the floor with a molecular model (suggesting that his aptitude for science is already developing).

While the parents want a healthy child, they dislike the idea of a totally predetermined baby. How does the geneticist respond to their concerns?

Caesar

Key quotes

'When you clean the glass, Vincent, don't clean it too well ... you might get ideas.' (**8d**)

Bearing an absurd name for a menial worker, Caesar's gentle mockery of Vincent's dreaming is kindly meant. His aim is to keep janitor Vincent focused on his lowly job. In fact, Caesar's jibes keep motivating Vincent to strive harder. His retort, 'Yeah, but if the glass is clean it'll be easier for you to see me when I'm on the other side of it' (**8d**), turns out to be incorrect. Caesar sees but doesn't recognise Vincent when he has become 'Mr Morrow' (**16f**).

THEMES, IDEAS & VALUES

Individuals in the real world absorb their culture's ways of thinking, but may also come to disagree with some aspects of what is generally accepted. Depending on a society's permitted freedom of expression, disagreements may lead to fierce public debate that can openly challenge an ideological position and may bring about societal changes.

Plays, novels and films are all shaped by in-built biases, beliefs and attitudes. A film is never neutral – it always carries an **ideological message**, even if that message is not blatantly obvious. What values are being set up and promoted in *Gattaca*? Consider some value-challenging scenarios in the film.

- How and why is Vincent able to outwit Gattaca's security controls? Should a character recognisable as a 'hero' lie his way to success? Yes, says the film, because Vincent has special qualities. What kind of personality is being given high value in the story then?
- What contrasting attitudes to life are expressed by Vincent, Jerome, Anton and Irene? Anton's personality is made unattractive – why?
- It seems that Lamar disagrees with the discriminatory system he's supposed to monitor, but he cannot speak out against it openly. So what does he do? He overrides the eugenic program. Perhaps, by the end of the film, Anton has also started to question the eugenic values he is supposed to police.
- Can Director Josef's crime of murder be justified? Does the film justify it? And how does the film lead viewers to think about social equality?

Questions such as these help you to identify values being put forward by the filmmakers.

Genetics and nature

Look back at the notes on **Genes and genetics**: genes are nature's building blocks for all life forms. Genetic manipulation is concerned with intervening in a natural process of DNA replicating itself in order to alter the outcome of that process. So genetics and nature might sometimes work in opposition to each other.

Geneticists intervene in the natural life-making process for many reasons, but the most acceptable and widely publicised research claims to be for the long-term benefit to people. Genetic research has already led to breakthroughs in the treatment of diseases. In the future it will make people healthier, live longer and so on. But will genetic advances make humans happier or alter possibly non-genetically determined aspects of individual personality?

Consider the film's basic arguments on this theme. Several key issues are being explored.

What is natural?

The opening epigraphs present two contrasting ideas about what is natural. The first expresses a fundamentally passive acceptance of nature as it comes, ordained by a divine Creator to be flawed sometimes. The idea seems to be that human intervention is pointless, even sacrilegious – who would dare to tamper with the way nature has been made?

> Consider God's handiwork: who can straighten what he hath made crooked? (Ecclesiastes 6.13).

The second epigraph presents the opposite view, but in an interestingly unscientific way.

> I not only think we will tamper with Mother Nature, I think Mother wants us to (Willard Gaylin).

Now nature is characterised as a Mother goddess, somehow urging human beings to intervene in natural processes to make life better.

Which view does the film support? The geneticist at the fertility clinic argues to Vincent's parents that their next son will be 'the best of you', a VALID with good life prospects: 'You could conceive a thousand times naturally and never get such a result' (**6a**).

Yet Anton (like Jerome, Irene and Lamar's son) is shown to be flawed in ways that Vincent, the naturally conceived 'faith birth' with a poor genetic profile, manages to overcome. The film confirms that there is no gene for fate, that chance and other unknown factors still play a part in a child's development and an adult's success.

Benefits of genetic engineering?

Vincent concedes that for the genetically superior, success is easier to attain but by no means guaranteed (**9a**). Jerome's DNA fashioned an Olympic swimmer who never achieves his true champion's capacity until he has to meet the challenge of hauling himself up the staircase at great speed to help Vincent. He could easily get into Gattaca, too, but lacks the desire to do so until Vincent's dream activates his own spirit to achieve.

The only person who has been genetically modified in an obvious way is the freakish 12-fingered pianist (**20a, e**), who is presented ambiguously in the film. Irene is impressed by his wonderful recital, informing Vincent that the version of the Schubert *Impromptu* they hear (with more notes) can be played only with 12 fingers. The Schubert piece in its original form can be played successfully by ten-fingered folk.

How does the pianist feel about his extra fingers? He makes an extraordinary gesture of peeling off his gloves and throwing them to an eager audience at the end, like a striptease artist. Vincent is appalled and fascinated by this man. We notice how the pianist has covered his face with his unusual hands in the poster. Is he ashamed of being a freak? Or are his hands the part of him that he values most?

What does it mean to be human?

The film suggests an approach to this question by showing us how people deal with life experiences and what qualities help or hinder their capacity to live fully. Being human for Vincent means acknowledging weakness and failure while still keeping his courage to take risks for good reasons. He's myopic but when circumstances make it necessary for him to lose his contact lenses, he still dares to cross a busy road blind (**21b**). He says he'll take his one chance in a hundred that there's nothing wrong with his heart (**7a**). He beats Anton in the two crucial swims because he doesn't hold anything back (**7c**, **33b**). Vincent's aspirations move him forward towards his dream, taking him through and beyond painful setbacks.

Jerome, too, overcomes his suicidal response to the shame of personal failure by finding human value in his life with Vincent, free from the VALID culture's anxiety-inducing expectation of excellence. A measure of his returning spirit is his sense of humour, especially when he counters Vincent's amazed, 'How the hell did you get up here?' with a joke about his crippled state, 'Oh, I could always walk – I've been faking it' (**29a**).

The key idea is that failure and weakness are part of the experience of being human. People can either be strengthened and use what they've learnt to make the future better (like Vincent, Jerome, Irene and Lamar, perhaps) or just appear tough and stay frightened (like Anton). Over the gate of the classical temple of Apollo at Delphi was written: 'Man know thyself and thou shalt know the universe.' This is an unspoken but fundamental idea in *Gattaca*.

Discrimination

It is possible to speak positively about a person 'having discrimination': it means that the person has qualities of judgement to distinguish carefully between two different things. Used in the negative sense, the word describes societal prejudice by the majority against minority groups in a community. 'We now have discrimination down to a science,' says Vincent (**8a**).

VALID and INVALID

These terms define the way people are coded. Children such as Vincent, born to non-compliant parents, are socially discriminated against by default, immediately identifiable on computer files as INVALIDS. They have limited access to schooling, take on low-status jobs, are denied training opportunities to fulfil greater aspirations and are harassed by the police. Vincent makes the journey from disadvantaged to successful only because he has the wit and courage to play a discriminatory system at its own game – he buys himself a genetically perfect 'ladder' who has no place as a VALID because he is crippled. Vincent knows that Jerome as a VALID, vitro, made man, suffers from another kind of discrimination – the burden of perfection (**12b**).

Resistance?

VALID compliance with the superior 'system' made to benefit VALIDS can't be assumed, since Jerome and Lamar actively subvert it, possibly joined by Director Josef, and German lives by trading across lines in VALID DNA. Also, there seems to be a thriving underground of people who have something to hide from the police: look at the panic when there is a raid on the Cavendish Club (**24b**).

Your body used in evidence against you

Discrimination is facilitated in Vincent's society by constant DNA surveillance. Every skin flake and hair you shed is liable to incriminate you. The film makes much of the intense physical activity on and in the human body, beginning with detailed scrutiny of Vincent's washing and cleaning routine.

People often feel embarrassed about discussing ordinary human body waste. We all wash, scrub, shave, pluck and snip to maintain our bodies, discarding the debris as something a bit shameful. Perhaps it's because it reminds us how human we really are, just a mass of active cells. Notice how the film draws attention to the following: spit, hair, eyelashes, blood, urine, vomit, saliva, sweat, skin flakes and nail clippings. Things normally disposed of become the important DNA samples to be preserved carefully by Jerome, working in his laboratory for Vincent's benefit.

Science and dreams

The word 'science' comes from the Latin word *scientia*, meaning 'knowledge'. Even though science is thought of as a rational activity of the conscious and trained mind, it is a fact that a number of scientific problems have been resolved after inspirational hints in the dreams of preoccupied researchers.

The dream of space exploration

The enquiring human mind is given to dreams and creative speculation – all of which yield knowledge of different kinds. For example, the mind of wheelchair-bound physicist Stephen Hawking comes up with theoretical speculations about the nature of phenomena such as black holes in deep space. In 1980, Carl Sagan, Professor of Astronomy and Space Sciences at Cornell University, presented astronomy to a wide audience in an exciting television series called *Cosmos*. Sagan's aim was to combine hard science with a visionary message for human beings about cosmic mysteries still to be discovered and a deeper respect for planet Earth. Science fiction still appeals as a genre because it deals with dreams beyond the limited space travel that is just beginning to be a scientific reality.

Vincent's dream is to go into space. When Jerome asks, 'Why? What's up there?' he answers, 'I don't know. That's what I want to find out …' (**11b**). And as he swims back with the defeated Anton, Vincent looks up at the stars, confident in his dream of getting there (**33b**).

Dreams of a better world created by science

Not all research is motivated by altruistic urges to realise human dreams and create a better world, free from disease, malnutrition, destruction of species and resources, land degradation and so on. Then again, not all science allied with biotech companies or the military is necessarily deplorable or nightmarish. Sometimes it is difficult for scientists to predict where science is heading or how their work will be applied by political leaders. The genetics debate that is in progress, for example, may have unforeseen positive and negative consequences for the future. *Gattaca* demonstrates how utopian dreams can turn into dystopian nightmares.

Name and identity

In everyday life, people are frequently asked to give their names – most do so without a second thought. If you were given a name you don't like, you can usually change it legally without too much effort, even if your family object. You may think your name suits your overall identity very well or that it doesn't represent how you see yourself at all – so you may prefer a nickname. On the internet, too, people disguise themselves with exotic codenames to chat with equally anonymous individuals.

In other times and places, a personal name or even a nickname, was held sacred, not something to be spoken, revealed easily, changed or given away, because it contained its owner's life force. The ancient Egyptians, for example, believed that to erase someone's written or carved name was to destroy that person's identity, making their anonymous soul unrecognisable to the gods.

Identity, then, is related to a name but goes beyond it to indicate everything that belongs to the human personality who owns the name, who is identified by it. A name identifies an individual. What are the distinguishing markers of personal identity? People carry different kinds of 'identity cards' bearing their photographs and signatures.

Passing on a family name to children

Vincent's father, Antonio, is reluctant to give his name to a sickly child and Vincent's VALID younger brother, Anton, is described as a son his father considered worthy of his name (**6b**). Because he is so aware that his family think him to be a chronically ill (**5c**) runt, Vincent erases his name from the humiliating measuring pole (**6b**). Later, after beating Anton at swimming, he literally tears his visual identity out of a family photograph before walking off into the night (**7d**).

Protecting your individual name

As he practises signing the name 'Jerome' with his right hand, left-handed Vincent comments, 'It's a good name,' to which Jerome replies sourly, 'It's my name. What makes you think that you can be me?' (**11a**). The film traces the delicate negotiation between Vincent and Jerome to share the name 'Jerome', which does not refer to an individual but to a composite Gattaca identity assumed by Vincent with Jerome's help.

> Eugene, I need you to be yourself for today, okay? … I was never very good at it, remember? (**28a, b**).

Vincent finally goes off to Titan with his own name, reclaimed and made VALID with Lamar's help (**35a**) and by Jerome's self-sacrifice (**36b**).

Defining a genetic identity

> When a member of the elite falls on hard times, their genetic identity becomes a valued commodity (**9a**).

Vincent, in fact, will not be what Jerome was in the past; he'll be better because he'll come first, and with Jerome's help, which means Jerome will also come first. Even as he appears to be obliterated, Jerome's genetic identity will survive, for he also goes into space.

Relationships

Whatever kind of domestic model or community groupings prevail in a culture, human individuals (even hermits) must relate somehow to other individuals. The ties that bind are complex. Bonds between parents and children, and between siblings, are often stressful or absent. Despite the old adage that 'blood is thicker than water' – which makes the assumption that there is 'natural closeness' in families – deeper loyalties may be found outside in friendships. *Gattaca* develops these ideas, showing too, that even in highly controlled and 'cool' emotional environments, adults strive to find friends and partners.

How bonded are blood relations?

Anxious parents predispose Vincent to feel like a runt and encourage Anton to feel superior. Vincent's final question, 'Are we brothers?' sounds like a final appeal to Anton's nature for brotherly support as opposed to following his official duty.

Future society

How will society develop in the future? This theme opens up many serious issues about state-monitoring of individuals and speculates on how far people are prepared to have their lives controlled. What will work be like in the future? The *Gattaca* scenario has a rigidly stratified labour force (VALIDS at the top and INVALIDS at the bottom). Will the trend be towards more social hierarchy or greater egalitarianism? Utopian or dystopian arguments can be explored here.

However future society develops, it is clear that Vincent wants to get away from a world he considers unsatisfactory: 'Maybe it was a love of the planets ... giving me a dislike of this one' (**6d**). Eugene echoes his view more strongly when the cop insults him by using the word 'cripple': 'I'm getting off this ball of dirt' (**20c**).

DIFFERENT INTERPRETATIONS

Different interpretations arise from different responses to a text. Over time, a text will give rise to a wide range of responses from its readers, who may come from various social or cultural groups and live in very different places and historical periods. These responses can be published in newspapers, journals and books by critics and reviewers or they can be expressed in discussions among readers in the media, classrooms, book groups and so on. While there is no single correct reading or interpretation of a text, it is important to understand that an interpretation is more than a personal opinion – it is the justification of a point of view on the text. To present an interpretation of the text based on your point of view you must use a logical argument and support it with relevant evidence from the text.

Two interpretations

The following two interpretations show how textual evidence and reasoning can be used to support two strongly contrasting views of *Gattaca*. Your own view could possibly combine elements of each or perhaps take a completely different view of the film's main themes and ideas.

Interpretation 1: *Gattaca* shows the triumph of the human spirit overcoming adversity.

This interpretation emphasises the positive elements of the world depicted by the film over the negative ones. Vincent lives in a society that regards his hopes and dreams as futile and meaningless; his genes are regarded as his destiny and he is denied any legitimate opportunity to improve his quality of life or to fulfil his ambitions. The gap between VALIDS and INVALIDS is ruthlessly enforced, using near universal methods of surveillance to monitor and regulate people's lives. Despite this, Vincent finds a way to become not merely a successful employee at Gattaca but an astronaut – achieving his childhood dream of travelling into space.

In a world in which so many aspects of life are measured and controlled – from education and employment to the choice of a partner – *Gattaca* celebrates the capacity of individuals to resist and subvert these forms of regulation and oppression. Vincent experiences physical pain (in having his legs lengthened) as well as the constant anxiety of knowing his deception might be discovered at any moment. He is also subjected to the constant assurances of others that he is not capable of success, that he is foolish even to dream: as his father says, 'The only way you'll see the inside of a spaceship is if you were cleaning it.' Even Anton cannot believe that Vincent can compete on equal terms with VALIDS, despite the clear evidence that Vincent can achieve whatever he sets his mind to.

If Vincent is the most obvious example of what the human spirit is capable of, he is by no means the only character to subvert the rules and regulations of society and of the Gattaca Corporation in particular. Jerome/Eugene, profoundly disillusioned, willingly breaks the law and testifies to the importance of dreams and aspirations: as he says to Vincent, 'I only lent you my body – you lent me your dream.' Lamar reveals at the end of the film that he has known of Vincent's deception for some time, but out of admiration for what Vincent has achieved and because Vincent provides an inspirational example for his son, he has taken no action. Irene finally dispenses with the need to know Vincent's true genetic makeup and assists in maintaining the fiction that Jerome/Vincent and Jerome/Eugene are one and the same person when Anton visits the apartment. Anton, too, plays his part in subverting the system, steering Detective Hugo away from performing a second round of blood tests that would surely expose Vincent's real identity. Perhaps Anton, though, is too much a product of the system, for he refuses to endorse Vincent's dream or help him achieve it.

Each of these characters finds moments in their lives when they must choose between the demands of the corporation they work for and their hopes and desires as individual human beings. *Gattaca* endorses their choices when they speak for freedom and individuality; for the right of humanity to dream and to accomplish those dreams.

Interpretation 2: *Gattaca* presents a bleak view of a society in which science determines human destinies.

This interpretation sees the film as depicting a society that is ultimately far more powerful than the individual. In many ways this is a less obvious reading than the one above – indeed, the tagline, 'There is no gene for the human spirit', clearly points to the victory of the individual over the oppressive system as the film's central story or message. However, it is also possible to see the film as a dire warning about what is possible; as a depiction of a world in which the laws of science, rather than the vagaries of human will and imagination, determine the course of lives.

Although Vincent becomes an astronaut despite all the forces of society working against him, his success can be viewed not as a 'win' against an oppressive society but as an endorsement of its values. Vincent becomes someone who does not seek to change society but conforms to it perfectly and shares in its valorisation of scientific methods. Even the tasks he performs to adopt the persona of 'Jerome' testify to the power of science: blood, tissue and urine samples are prepared with all the technical skill and dedication of a chemist or doctor in a domestic laboratory.

None of Vincent's actions place any pressure on the operations of the rigid class system, the discrimination against INVALIDS, the extreme reliance on genetic information: the system as a whole does not even notice Vincent's subversive presence. Jerome/Eugene puts it succinctly: 'When they look at you, they don't see you any more, they see me.' Vincent evades the system, but he does not change it; nor does the film suggest any way in which this systematic oppression and discrimination might be changed, let alone overthrown.

Vincent's dream comes true, but only because it is so consistent with the aims and values of the society he lives in, and because he is talented in a way that this society recognises – scientific ability. For other kinds of talent, for other dreams, this world seems to have no place. Even the pianist has been 'perfected' by science and the experience of music in his recital is as much about witnessing the marvel of science as sharing in the magic of human creativity and expression. *Gattaca* shows a world in which people still have individual desires and aspirations, but which mercilessly suppresses those human traits unless they accord with the needs of the corporation or society as a whole.

QUESTIONS & ANSWERS

This section focuses on your own analytical writing on the text, and gives you strategies for producing high-quality responses in your coursework and exam essays.

Essay writing – an overview

An essay is a formal and serious piece of writing that presents your point of view on the text, usually in response to a given essay topic. Your 'point of view' in an essay is your interpretation of the meaning of the text's language, structure, characters, situations and events, supported by detailed analysis of textual evidence.

Analyse – don't summarise

In your essay it is important to avoid simply summarising what happens in a text:

- A **summary** is a description or paraphrase (retelling in different words) of the characters and events. For example: 'Macbeth has a horrifying vision of a dagger dripping with blood before he goes to murder King Duncan'.
- An **analysis** is an explanation of the real meaning or significance that lies 'beneath' the text's words (and images, for a film). For example: 'Macbeth's vision of a bloody dagger shows how deeply uneasy he is about the violent act he is contemplating – as well as his sense that supernatural forces are impelling him to act'.

A limited amount of summary is sometimes necessary to let your reader know which part of the text you wish to discuss. However, always keep this to a minimum and follow it immediately with your analysis (explanation) of what this part of the text is really telling us.

Plan your essay

Carefully plan your essay so that you have a clear idea of what you are going to say. The plan ensures that your ideas flow logically, that your argument remains consistent and that you stay on the topic. An essay plan should be a list of **brief dot points** – no more than half a page. It includes:

- your central argument or main contention – a concise statement (usually in a single sentence) of your overall response to the topic (see 'Analysing a sample topic' for guidelines on how to formulate a main contention)
- three or four dot points for each paragraph indicating the main idea and evidence/examples from the text – note that in your essay you will need to *expand* on these points and *analyse* the evidence.

Structure your essay

An essay is a complete, self-contained piece of writing. It has a clear beginning (the introduction), middle (several body paragraphs) and end (the last paragraph or conclusion). It must also have a central argument that runs throughout, linking each paragraph to form a coherent whole.

See examples of introductions and conclusions in the 'Analysing a sample topic' and 'Sample answer' sections.

The introduction establishes your overall response to the topic. It includes your main contention and outlines the main evidence you will refer to in the course of the essay. Write your introduction after you have done a plan and before you write the rest of the essay.

The body paragraphs argue your case – they present evidence from the text and explain how this evidence supports your argument. Each body paragraph needs:

- a strong **topic sentence** (usually the first sentence) that states the main point being made in the paragraph
- **evidence** from the text, including some brief quotations
- **analysis** of the textual evidence, explaining its significance, and an **explanation** of how it supports your argument
- **links back to the topic** in one or more statements, usually towards the end of the paragraph.

Connect the body paragraphs so that your discussion flows smoothly. Use some linking words and phrases, such as 'similarly' and 'on the other hand', though don't start every paragraph like this. Another strategy is to use a significant word from the last sentence of one paragraph in the first sentence of the next.

Use key terms from the topic – or synonyms for them – throughout, so the relevance of your discussion to the topic is always clear.

The conclusion ties everything together and finishes the essay. It includes strong statements that emphasise your central argument and provide a clear response to the topic.

Avoid simply restating the points made earlier in the essay – this will end on a very flat note and imply that you have run out of ideas and vocabulary. The conclusion is meant to be a logical extension of what you have written, not just a repetition or summary of it. Writing an effective conclusion can be a challenge. Try using these tips:

- Start by linking back to the final sentence of the second-last paragraph – this helps your writing to 'flow', rather than just leaping back to your main contention straight away.
- Use synonyms and expressions with equivalent meanings to vary your vocabulary. This allows you to reinforce your line of argument without being repetitive.
- When planning your essay, think of one or two broad statements or observations about the text's wider meaning. These should be related to the topic and your overall argument. Keep them for the conclusion, since they will give you something 'new' to say, but still follow logically from your discussion. The introduction will be focused on the topic, but the conclusion can present a wider view of the text.

Essay topics

1. 'One man's loss is another man's gain,' says Vincent, moments before the viewer first meets Jerome. Does the film show this view about success and failure to be true, considering how their relationship develops?
2. How does crime structure the plot development in *Gattaca*?
3. Compare and contrast how the relationships between Vincent and his two very different 'brothers', Anton and Jerome, are defined in terms of swimming.
4. How significant is Michael Nyman's music in shaping the viewer's response to key scenes?
5. How and why does the film's *mise en scène* create different visual environments for Vincent and Anton, Vincent and Jerome, and Jerome/Vincent and Irene?
6. How specifically does the editing of segment **28** (**Who is Jerome?**) contribute to the narrative suspense and how is that suspense resolved?
7. 'If you're still interested, let me know', say Irene and Jerome/Vincent at different times. Is there any room for love or trust in relationships structured around an organisation like *Gattaca*?

8 'We now have discrimination down to a science.' Discrimination, either positive or negative, is inevitable in any society because people are individuals and therefore different. Discuss.

9 *Gattaca* shows that even if your resumé is in your genes, what you make of your life is up to you. Do you agree?

10 'That's how I did it, Anton. I never saved anything for the swim back.' Vincent defies and transcends his destiny and, in doing so, inspires others. Discuss.

Vocabulary for writing on *Gattaca*

Cut: A type of film edit that enables shots to follow one another with no noticeable gap.

Dissolve: A type of film edit in which there is a brief overlap between one shot and the next.

DNA: Abbreviation for deoxyribonucleic acid, a large molecule in the shape of a double helix; contains all the genetic information of an organism.

Dystopia: A fictional world that is cruel and oppressive, severely limiting human happiness and freedom.

Eugenics: The science and practice of attempting to improve the genetic makeup of a population by identifying desirable characteristics, selective breeding, removing individuals from a population etc.

Film noir: Film genre typically used for detective stories; features dark lighting, shadows, hard surfaces, a black-and-white or monochromatic colour scheme and usually an urban setting; strongly associated with 1950s America.

Flashback: A shift back in time to recount an earlier part of the narrative. In *Gattaca*, there is a flashback from the film's 'present' to depict Vincent's childhood and the events in his life that have led up to this point.

Gene: A sequence of DNA; can be linked with a particular inherited trait, such as eye colour.

Genetic engineering: The process of manipulating genetic material (e.g. by inserting new genetic material) to produce different characteristics in an organism.

Genome: The complete genetic material of an organism.

Mise en scène: Everything that appears within the frame at any given moment; includes setting, lighting, costumes and acting style.
Science fiction: Fictional genre (including film) set in the future, usually imagining forms of technology that are yet to be invented or mastered (e.g. manned space travel to other planets).
Voice-over: A narrative voice that accompanies the action to give context and continuity; in *Gattaca*, Jerome/Vincent provides occasional narrative voice-overs, such as just before the flashback to his childhood and at the end of the film.

Analysing a sample topic

'If you're still interested, let me know,' say Irene and Jerome/Vincent at different times. Is there any room for love or trust in relationships structured around an organisation like Gattaca?
Notice, there's a quote to start with, so you should immediately think about where and when the two characters say the line in the film.

Introduce your discussion by referring to the significance of the quote for the lovers, both of whom are Gattaca employees. Your focus will be Jerome/Vincent and Irene, backed up by a few secondary characters. You should also note briefly that you are going to exclude Jerome/Eugene from this discussion (although he is a central character in the film and has been engineered for a Gattaca career) because he is never directly part of the Gattaca system.

Irene says the line after admitting that she's had Jerome/Vincent sequenced (**17**) to check out his suitability as a potential partner. She gives Jerome/Vincent one of her hairs so that he can check out her less perfect DNA profile and he gallantly lets it blow away in the wind. The approved clinical response would be to check her DNA profile, too, but he doesn't – you can suggest why not.

You could argue that Vincent already knows that DNA profiles predict very little about how someone turns out. He is motivated by a natural desire for Irene.

Irene does the same thing in return when Jerome/Vincent has confessed who he really is and offers her one of his own hairs to sequence with the repeated line (**34a**). Again, suggest why she lets the hair blow away.

You could argue that Irene, born with all the expectations of being a VALID (but suffering the shame of being flawed, which is reinforced at Gattaca), starts out as more anxious to check her partner but finally learns to judge Jerome/Vincent by his character rather than his DNA. What finally convinces her?

You may come to the conclusion that because they are shown to be falling in love, they are interested in seeing each other as more than simply bundles of desirable or faulty DNA. And so they are prepared to trust in a 'natural' human partnership, whatever the result may be.

Move on to the next part of the question, which implies that Gattaca's values foster non-loving or mistrustful relationships. Start with Vincent's comment about a child conceived in love (**5a**).

Vincent's parents, who conceived Vincent in love and trust, are labelled as irresponsible for blighting their first son's chances of a Gattaca career. Mistrustful of their own natural impulses, they rely on professional assistance to design their second son, the VALID Anton. Appropriately, he becomes Gattaca's security chief, from which position he can better calm his deep neurotic fears of being challenged by INVALIDS by policing the system.

Find instances in the film where the emotionless clinical placidity that characterises Gattaca's workers on the surface is contrasted with strong feelings still existing underneath the designer suits and lab coats. However carefully they try to conceal feelings, Gattaca's personnel are not robots.

You could comment on Director Josef (murderer), Lamar (concealer of information) and Irene's impulse, despite her suspicions, to warn Jerome/Vincent. Your conclusion might be that within Gattaca there are people who are subverting the coldly efficient system – for its own good, finally.

In your conclusion you could emphasise that although Gattaca is a hard environment for VALIDS, designed to promote competition and mutual surveillance, it employs key individuals who deliberately work against it.

Finish by suggesting that through love and trust, Jerome/Vincent and Irene may return to the old way of conceiving children who will be valued (by their parents at least) as much by personal characteristics as by their genetic inheritance. This may be a romantic and scientifically naive idea but it seems to be where the film is heading for closure on the relationship.

SAMPLE ANSWER

'That's how I did it, Anton. I never saved anything for the swim back.' Vincent defies and transcends his destiny and, in doing so, inspires others. Discuss.

Destined to be an INVALID but driven to rebel, Vincent's bravery and determination help him surpass his predetermined potential. He proves the falsity of genetic determinism. His victory over his fate encourages and gives hope to people with their own genetic problems, such as Irene and Doctor Lamar, and his defiant courage and perseverance inspire others, too.

Images of barriers stress the hurdles of class and discrimination that Vincent must overcome – the gate shutting in the child Vincent's face; the glass barriers through which Vincent the cleaner watches the employees inside Gattaca; the cyclone fences that segregate the INVALIDS from the VALIDS; the shots inside Vincent's childhood home isolating him from the rest of the family. But Vincent is somebody who won't 'accept the hand he's been dealt,' who rejects his INVALID genetic destiny.

Vincent disappoints his father yet refuses to see himself as inferior, urging Anton to become his blood brother and swimming against him. Winning the race makes him doubt the caste system and whole ideology of genetic determinism: 'My brother was not as strong as he believed and I was not as weak.' He realises anything is possible with courage, persistence and spirit. Refusing to submit to their negative view of him, Vincent leaves his family.

Vincent's heroic dedication is shown in his efforts to transcend his genetic self and disguise himself as 'Jerome'. Shots of him scrubbing himself stress his constant struggle to overcome his genetic inheritance, to erase his real identity and construct a false one, while, ironically, forging an authentic and strong identity or individuality. Although faking genetic tests, Jerome/Vincent passes every real test of strength, courage and character.

He demonstrates this courage when he risks swimming beyond Anton and his physical potential, when he has his legs stretched, and when he crosses the highway blind. That success, where his desire to reach Irene conquers his physical weakness in allowing him to overcome his defective vision, exemplifies his will to overcome all defects.

Vincent's defects give him the spirit Jerome/Eugene and the others lack. Inner strength can't be engineered as it emerges out of an individual contending with the challenges of a specific environment. Someone engineered with no flaws, such as Jerome/Eugene, lacks the strength of character Vincent develops through his struggle to overcome his genetic heritage. Jerome/Vincent represents a flawed human spirit's victory over perfect, genetically engineered society.

In proving that genes aren't the sole determinant of people's lives, Vincent inspires and changes others. Caesar sees him inside Gattaca as a top-rung employee; admiring Jerome/Vincent's audacity, he keeps his secret and protects him against the police. Jerome/Vincent's rise allows other INVALIDS to hope for more than genetic inferiority.

He wins Irene's admiration and devotion when she learns how he's battled his way up, proving that she needn't submit to the fate dictated by her faulty heart. She recognises the bravery that subverts the system's definition of him: 'You couldn't see, could you? ... You crossed anyway.' When Irene releases the hair he offers her for testing, this 'letting go' suggests she discards and frees herself from her belief in genetic determinism and its demand of perfection. Instead, she accepts both the 'natural' Vincent and herself.

Vincent also encourages Doctor Lamar and his son to reject the destiny that genetics has supposedly determined for the boy: '...a big fan of yours ... Unfortunately, my son's not as good as they promised ... but then who knows what he could do.'

Above all, Vincent inspires Jerome/Eugene, helping him (temporarily) overcome his bitterness at not living up to the expectations created by perfect genes. First deriding him ('What makes you think that you can be me?'), Eugene later admits, 'You were always better at being me.' He sees that unenhanced Vincent is better at being 'Jerome' than Jerome/Eugene himself. Vincent has built a genuinely strong character – paradoxically, by remaining true to himself. Jerome/Eugene recognises this integrity when he drunkenly calls him 'Vincent'.

Jerome/Eugene eventually identifies with Vincent's struggle – 'I only lent you my body. You lent me your dream'– and this transforms him. When he drags himself up the staircase to pose as 'Jerome' before Anton, he transcends his fate as a cripple. Inspired by his friend, Jerome/Eugene finally wins a race, 'swimming' up the stairs to pass a real test of character – something he never managed as a genetically engineered champion. Jerome/Eugene's bravery here parallels that of Vincent crossing the road blind. Vincent has transmitted his courage to Jerome/Eugene – his 'borrowed ladder' borrows his spirit.

The fires from Vincent's rocket at the end blend with the fire in the incinerator – Jerome/Eugene has become 'one' with Jerome/Vincent. Jerome/Vincent helped Jerome/Eugene escape self-absorbed cynicism. Proving 'there's no gene for fate', he transforms and inspires many during his 'journey' to the stars.

REFERENCES & READING

Amis, K. 1961, *New Maps of Hell: A Survey of Science Fiction,* Victor Gollancz, London. (See Chapter 3, 'New light on the unconscious'.)

Appleyard, B. 2000, *Brave New Worlds: Genetics and the Human Experience,* Harper Collins, London.

Bordwell, D. and Thompson, K. 2001, *Film Art: An Introduction,* McGraw Hill, New York. (Contains a full glossary of film terms and detailed notes on reading film.)

Fowles, J. 2001, *The Aristos,* Vintage, London.

Griffiths, J. 1980, *Three Tomorrows: American, British and Soviet Science Fiction,* Macmillan, London. (See Chapter 5, 'Utopia and dystopia'.)

Huxley, A. 1932, *Brave New World*, Chatton and Windus, London.

Nossal, G.J.V. 1984, *Reshaping Life: Key Issues in Genetic Engineering*, Melbourne University Press, Australia. (A clear introduction to genetic coding and the double helix.)

Sagan, C. 1980, *Cosmos*, Random House, New York.

The Map of Life 2001, sound recording, ABC Radio, Sydney. Featuring Professor Peter Doherty at the National Library of Australia.

Reviews and articles

Sight and Sound, March 1998, vol.8/3, pp.48–49. (Provocative review)

Websites

http://www.dnaftb.org – A most informative website on DNA.

http://www.genome.gov/18016863 – A brief guide to genomics.

http://bioethics.com/?page_id=8630 – A discussion on the ethical implications of the Human Genome Project, with links to other relevant topics.

http://www.nhmrc.gov.au/_files_nhmrc/publications/attachments/e39.pdf – A paper on the ethical aspects of human genetic testing.